Christ's Kids Create II

100 Creative Craft Projects, Group Activities, and Recipes
for children 4–14 years old

Compiled by Vicki Boston and Deborah Stroh
Illustrated by Deborah Stroh
Editor: Jane Haas
Editorial Assistant: Beverly J. Stroup

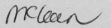

© 1993 Concordia Publishing House

CONTENTS

© 1993 Concordia Publishing House

Introduction

She was so proud of her art work. She had labored over it at home, wanting to impress her teacher. She waited patiently through the day for art class. The time finally came. She proudly pulled her picture out of her desk to show her teacher.

"You didn't do this!"

"Yes sir, I did it all by myself. I worked on it at home."

"No . . . you can't draw like this. Your mom helped you."

Then, to her horror, he tore up her beautiful picture and threw it away.

He thought she could not draw. And so she did not draw for years.

Then one day a substitute teacher saw her doodling and asked, "Why aren't you in my art class?" Her response was, "I can't draw."

She still tells herself, "I can't draw," but now she says this during a slump while illustrating children's books.

Were you this child? Maybe not in art, but in some other area. We, as teachers, do not always realize the affect we have on children. Our words need to be encouraging and honest, allowing children to freely use the talents God has given them.

Some children need a starting point and directions to follow. Other children need only the starting point.

As your craft time progresses, encourage individuality in the children. Be sensitive to each child's abilities. Celebrate the uniqueness of each child's work. Just think . . . 15 children making the same craft could result in 15 very different crafts. What a successful project!

To enable your craft time to be the most it can be, creative and filled with variety, ask parents and congregational members for materials. Get the word out! What word? Get the word out that you collect! Collect what? Spools, wooden blocks, lids—everything from A to Z.

Children today are taught to reduce, reuse, and recycle. Through these craft projects you will help them reuse and recycle.

A special thanks to Suzanne Hirth for her ideas.

Vicki Boston

Printing • • • • • • • • • • • • • •
on paper
　　wood
　　cardboard
with sponges
　　vegetables
　　fruits
　　cookie cutters
　　hands
　　feet
　　objects

Rubbings • • • • • • • • • • • •
use crayons
　　pencils
　　chalk
over sandpaper shapes
　　cardboard shapes
　　outside textures
　　sidewalks
　　bark
　　brick
　　stone
　　wood
inside textures
　　carpet
　　chair seats
　　walls
　　tables
　　fabric

Collages • • • • • • • • • • • •
anything cotton
　　lace
　　ribbon
　　paper
　　buttons
　　shells
　　sticks
　　feathers
　　spools
　　leaves

　　gravel
　　rocks
　　sequins
　　sponges
　　wallpaper
　　sawdust

on anything

　　nuts
　　seeds
　　bark
　　bottle caps
　　gum wrappers
　　coffee grounds
　　confetti
　　corks
　　crepe paper
　　fabric
　　glitter
　　straw
　　tiles
　　wood scraps
　　yarn
　　noodles

Stitchery • • • • • • • • • • • •
use yarn
　　ribbon
　　beads
　　string
　　feathers
　　twigs
on Styrofoam plates
　　meat trays
　　plastic mesh
　　cardboard
　　branches

Crayons • • • • • • • • • • • • •
(remove the paper and break them)
on paper plates
　　boxes
　　cups

　　wood
　　sandpaper
　　various shapes
　　of paper
Use a warming tray, cover it with
paper.
Draw a picture or design—try crayon
resist—paint over your crayoned
picture with watercolors

Tissue Paper • • • • • • • • •
　　torn
　　cut
　　wadded
use starch
　　watered-down glue
on paper
　　waxed paper
　　plates
　　cups
　　boxes

Chalk • • • • • • • • • • • • • •
on sandpaper
　　wet, dry paper
　　coffee filters
　　paper towels
use water
　　sugar water
　　buttermilk

Paint • • • • • • • • • • • • • •
on anything
　　with gelatin
　　　watercolors
　　　finger paint
　　　corn syrup with
　　　food coloring
　　Mix with sand
　　　cornmeal
　　　sawdust
　　　glue

Use brushes
　　sticks
　　cotton swabs
　　marbles
　　toothbrushes
　　vegetable brushes
　　feathers

Sculpture • • • • • • • • • • • •
use clay
　　junk
　　boxes
　　wood
　　Styrofoam
　　toothpicks
　　straws
with wood glue
　　craft glue

Murals/Banners • • • • • • • •
on paper
　　cardboard
　　plastic
　　felt
Use paint
　　torn paper
　　marking pens
　　crayons
　　collage materials

CRAFT
PROJECTS

Doily Butterfly

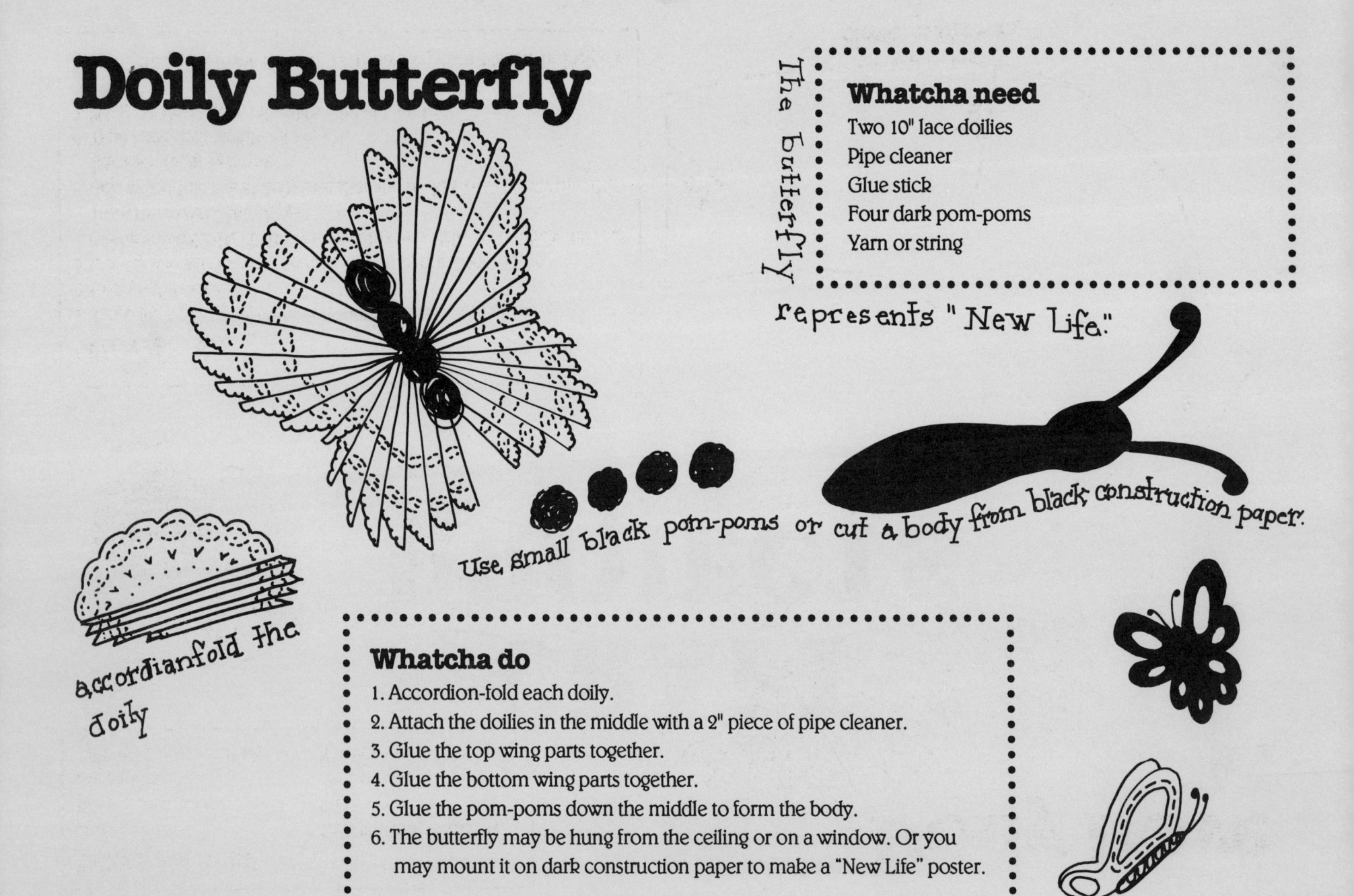

Whatcha need

Two 10" lace doilies
Pipe cleaner
Glue stick
Four dark pom-poms
Yarn or string

represents "New Life."

Use small black pom-poms or cut a body from black construction paper.

Accordianfold the doily

Whatcha do

1. Accordion-fold each doily.
2. Attach the doilies in the middle with a 2" piece of pipe cleaner.
3. Glue the top wing parts together.
4. Glue the bottom wing parts together.
5. Glue the pom-poms down the middle to form the body.
6. The butterfly may be hung from the ceiling or on a window. Or you may mount it on dark construction paper to make a "New Life" poster.

Doily Dove

Whatcha need

Dove pattern
White poster board
Scissors
One 10" white lace doily

One 8" white lace doily
Tape
Hole punch
Yarn or string

tape

yarn

hole punch

Scissors

Whatcha do

1. Trace the dove pattern onto the poster board.
2. Cut out the dove.
3. Cut the two slits into the dove as shown in the diagram.
4. Accordion-fold the 10" doily and slide the middle of the doily into the front slit, making the wings.
5. Accordion-fold the 8" doily and slide the middle of the doily into the back slit, making the tail.
6. Tape each doily lightly into place.
7. Hang the dove from the ceiling or light fixture.

Note: Christians use the dove as a symbol for peace and the Holy Spirit.

cut

cut

dove pattern

7

A Bowl Lot of Fun

coffee can or

coffee filters

bowl

pan for starch

liquid starch

food coloring

eye dropper

paper towels

Work on waxed paper

add grass and Easter eggs or flowers

Whatcha need

Coffee filters

Liquid starch

Paper towels

Bowl or coffee can

Waxed paper

Food coloring (4 drops per $\frac{1}{2}$ cup water)

Eyedropper

Whatcha do

1. Dip a coffee filter into the liquid starch.
2. Pull out the coffee filter and gently wipe off the excess starch.
3. Set the bowl or coffee can upside down on a sheet of waxed paper. Lay the filter over the inverted bowl or can.
4. Drip various colors of food coloring onto the coffee filter. Let it dry overnight.
5. When dry, remove the formed filter from the bowl or can.
6. Use the bowl to serve Blessing Cookies (page 80), or to serve your snack or the day.

Painted Burlap Banner

Whatcha need

Plain paper
Burlap, approximately 6" x 12"
Cardboard
Masking tape
Tempera paints
Liquid detergent
Paintbrush
Dowel or straw

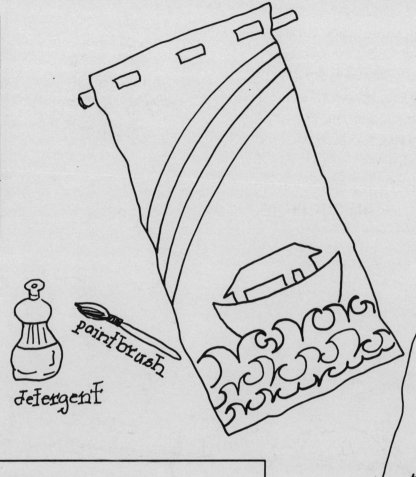

dowel or straw

masking tape

tempera paint

detergent

paintbrush

Whatcha do

1. Design a banner on plain paper.
2. Tape the burlap onto the cardboard. Stretch the burlap so there is no puckering.
3. Add 2 tablespoons liquid detergent to each $\frac{1}{2}$ cup of paint.
4. Paint your design onto the burlap. Allow to dry thoroughly.
5. $\frac{1}{2}$" from the top, start pulling out threads of burlap. Pull out 5–8 threads.
6. Weave the dowel or straw through the remaining threads.

9

Block Puzzle

Whatcha need

Four blocks of wood, 2" x 3" x 2"
Sandpaper
Plain paper, 8" x 12"
String or yarn
Tempera paint
Paintbrush
Brown shoe polish (paste, not liquid)
Soft cloth
Clear acrylic spray

Note: This project could be nicely framed with the slat frame.
See directions for Slat Frames on page 00.

Whatcha do

1. Sand the blocks of wood to eliminate any rough edges.
2. Draw a simple picture, such as a rainbow, clouds, and grass on the plain paper.
3. Fold the picture in half and in half again, so that when it is opened, it will be divided into four equal parts vertically. Each quarter section will be painted onto a side of the four blocks.
4. Place the four blocks on top of each other and tie with a string or yarn to keep them together.
5. Lay the blocks down and draw ¼ of the picture on each side of the blocks.
6. Paint the picture onto the wooden blocks, removing the string from sides 1 and 3 after sides 2 and 4 have been painted. When dry, tie the string going up and around sides 2 and 4 to paint sides 1 and 3. Let dry.
7. Remove the string completely and discard.
8. Use a soft cloth to lightly rub brown shoe polish over all sides of the cubes to give them a stained look.
9. Spray with acrylic spray. (An adult should do this in an area away from children.)

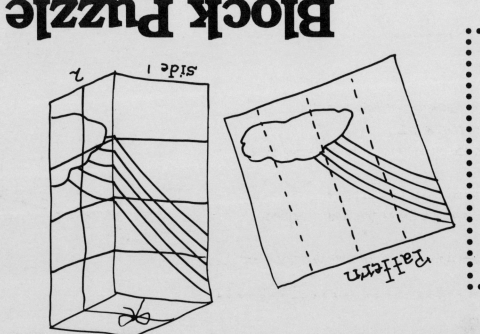

side 1

Pattern

string

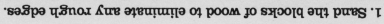

Paintbrush

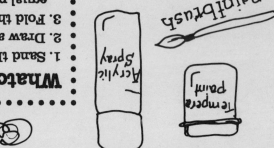

Acrylic Spray

Tempera Paint

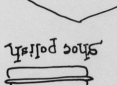

Shoe polish

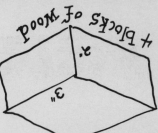

3"

2"

4 blocks of wood

Foil Fun

Whatcha need
- Junk (nails, paper clips, tokens, bolts, sticks, pencil stubs, bottle caps)
- Heavy cardboard
- Glue
- Aluminum foil
- Shoe polish (paste, not liquid)
- Soft cloth

Whatcha do
1. Collect small junk items.
2. Glue the items to a piece of heavy cardboard in the desired shape.
3. Tear a piece of foil 2" larger than the cardboard.
4. Gently press the foil over your junk sculpture to fit the form, being careful not to tear the foil.
5. Glue the foil to the back of the cardboard to keep it in place.
6. Rub shoe polish, using a soft cloth, over the foil to give it an antiqued look.

Note: This project looks good with a slat frame around it. See directions for making the slat frame on page 15.

11

Heart Headband

Decorate your headband with craft paints, beads, sequins - - - - - - -

Whatcha do

1. Cut two 2" x 12" strips of felt.
2. Fold one of the strips like a fan three times.
3. Trace the heart pattern on this page onto the first folded section. Cut the pattern, remembering not to cut through the folded ends.
4. Repeat steps 2 and 3 with the second strip of felt.
5. To connect the two strips to wear as a headband, cut the end of each strip as shown and hook the ends together.

Note: For smaller heads, you may have to cut off a heart at one end and then make the cuts to hook them together.

This project can also be done with crosses.

Whatcha need

Felt

Scissors

Celebration Stick

fold over

fold over

Continue folding over to build an accordian stack.

3.

2.

staple or tape

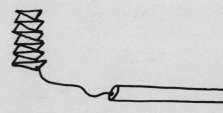

fold

Staple to yarn, then to a straw.

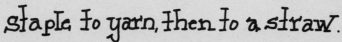

1.

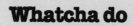

straw

yarn

Whatcha do

1. Cut two different colors of construction paper in two 1½" x 18" strips. If using wrapping paper, cut two 3" x 24" strips and fold in half lengthwise.
2. Staple or tape the two strips of paper together at one end to form an L shape.
3. Fold the strips, one over the other, until you reach the end.
4. Staple one end of the yarn to the top of the folded strips.
5. Staple the other end of the yarn to the straw. Use the straw as a handle.
6. You might want to staple ribbons to the bottom of the folded strips.

Note: Use your celebration stick for a joyous celebration of God's love, a birthday, Baptism, Easter party, parade, or a closing program.

13

Whatcha need

- One 8" x 10" piece of cardboard
- Aluminum foil
- Black (or dark) tempera paint
- Liquid detergent
- Nail
- Soft cloth or tissue

Be careful not to tear the foil as you work.

FOIL

foil

paintbrush

Black

Jesus

Foil Scratch

Whatcha do

1. Cover the cardboard with aluminum foil. (You may want to wrinkle the foil slightly first.)
2. Add 2 teaspoons liquid detergent to ½ cup tempera paint.
3. Paint the foil all over. Let dry.
4. Using the nail, gently (so as not to tear the aluminum) scrape off the paint to form a word, phrase, or picture.
5. If you wrinkled the foil, you may want to take a tissue or soft cloth and gently rub off some of the paint from the wrinkled raised aluminum.

Note: This project could be nicely framed with the slat frame. See directions for slat frames on page 15.

Slat Frame

Whatcha need

Two 12" wooden slats
Two 10" wooden slats
Craft glue or a glue gun
Puff paints or colored glue
Clear acrylic spray

Glue

Paint

Acrylic Spray

Decorate with shells, buttons, puzzle pieces, seeds, or nuts.

Whatcha do

1. Glue the four slats at the corners to form a frame. (Lay down the two 12" slats. Then glue the 10" slats to the top and bottom of the 12" sides to make an 8" x 10" opening.)
2. Decorate with puff paints or colored glue.
3. Spray with acrylic spray. **(An adult should do this outdoors in a well ventilated area, away from children.)**

♡ Jesus loves ♡

Samantha

Two by Two

animal crackers

pin back

glue gun

Acrylic Spray

Whatcha need

Two animal crackers
Craft paint (optional)
Glue gun
Clear acrylic spray
Pin backs

Whatcha do

1. Paint the animals crackers with craft paint.
2. Glue the two like animals together, one following the other. Let dry.
3. Spray with acrylic spray. **(An adult should do this outdoors in a well ventilated area, away from children.)** Let dry.
4. Glue on the pin backs. **(An adult should use the glue gun.)**

Variation: Paint the animals with brightly colored fingernail polish.

Cinnamon Stick Sculpture

Great Christmas ornaments.

Try a star shape

Whatcha need

Waxed paper
Cinnamon sticks
Glue gun
Raffia

cinnamon sticks

glue gun

Hang on the wall to remind you of

Christ — smells good.

Whatcha do

1. On waxed paper, lay out the cinnamon sticks in a desired shape (star, cross, triangle).
2. Glue the ends together with a glue gun. **(Have an adult use the glue gun.)**
3. Tie the joints with raffia to reinforce the glued areas.

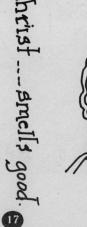

17

Stained-Glass Goodies

Whatcha need

Plastic milk cartons
Scissors
Permanent markers
Hole punch
Yarn

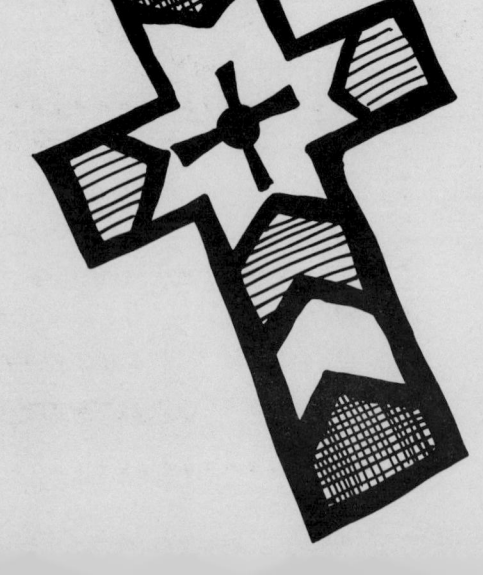

Whatcha do

1. Cut shapes from the sides of plastic milk cartons. **(Adult help is needed.)**
2. Outline the shape with permanent black marker. You may want to add black lines to give it a stained glass look.
3. Fill in between the black lines with other colors of markers.
4. Punch a hole in the top and hang in a window or in front of a light.

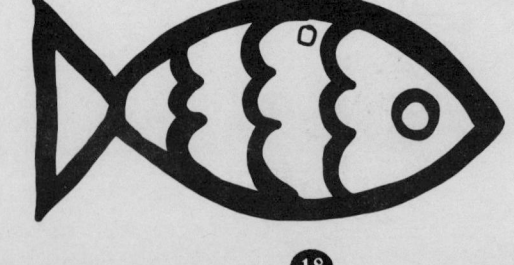

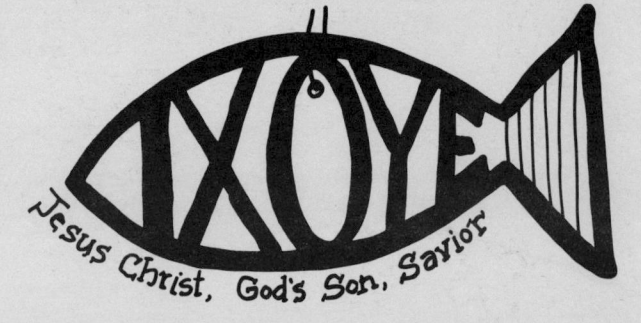

Jesus Christ, God's Son, Savior

Whatcha need

- Pinking shears
- Fabric
- Fabric paints or puff paints
- Glue gun
- Needle
- Embroidery thread

Treasure Bag

paint

Whatcha do

1. Use the pinking shears to cut the fabric into a 4" x 12" rectangle.
2. On the top half of the rectangle, paint a decoration or symbol. Let dry.
3. Fold the bottom half back and use a glue gun to attach the sides, front to back. (Have an adult use the glue gun.)
4. Thread the needle with 4 strands of embroidery thread.
5. Stitch around the top of the bag, starting at the front, 1" from the top; leave 3" to 4" of thread at each end.
6. Tie a knot in each end of the thread to keep if from pulling through.
7. Place your goodies in the bag and use the thread as a drawstring. Tie a bow to close your package.

Shave crayons with a cheese grater or the edge of a scissors.

scissors

waxed paper

cheese grater

an iron

Stained Hands

Whatcha do

1. Trace your hand (fingers together) on a piece of black construction paper. Cut it out—it will look like praying hands.
2. On one piece of waxed paper, center the praying hands.
3. Scatter crayon shavings around the hands.
4. Place a second piece of waxed paper over the shavings and hands.
5. Carefully place the design between several sheets of newspaper.
6. Press gently with a warm steam iron until the crayon shavings melt.
7. Make a frame by cutting out the center of black construction paper. Hang your stained hands in a window.

Note: Use a cheese grater or the edge of a scissors to shave crayons.

Noah's Animals in a Cage

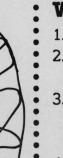

Whatcha do

1. Blow up the balloon.
2. Dip the string or yarn into white glue; wrap it around the balloon many times until it resembles a cage. Let dry overnight.
3. Pop the balloon and remove its pieces from the cage. **(For safety to children and animals, be sure to throw away *all* pieces of the balloon.)**
4. Punch a hole at the top of the animal; hang it by a string from the top inside of the cage.
5. Tie a string at the top of the cage to hang it.
6. Hang all the animal cages in one area for your "zoo" of animals.

Bug Box

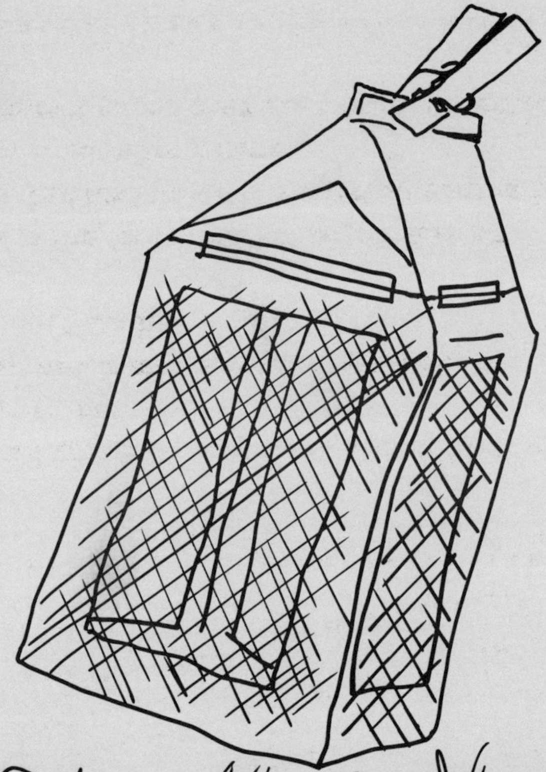

Whatcha need

Half gallon or quart milk carton
Scissors
Old nylon pantyhose
Tape
Clothespins

Whatcha do

1. Cut out all four sides of the milk carton, leaving the corners intact.
2. Cut the legs off a pair of old pantyhose. Pull a leg up from the bottom of the milk carton; tape it just above the "windows."
3. Leave the top open to put in God's small creatures.
4. Close the top with clothespins. Observe.
5. Leave the small creature in the box only long enough to enjoy and watch. Let the creature(s) out at the end of class so they can go back to nature to do the jobs God gave them to do.

Puzzling Thoughts of God's Creation

Whatcha need

- Four empty juice boxes
- Plain wrapping paper or tissue paper
- Tape
- Scissors
- Full page magazine pictures (from zoo newsletters, *National Geographic, Your Big Backyard* magazines)
- Glue
- Clear contact paper (*optional*)

cut

magazine

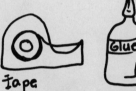

wrapping paper

tape

Glue

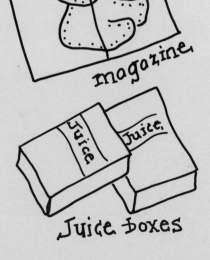

Juice boxes

Whatcha do

1. Wrap each juice box with wrapping paper or several layers of tissue paper, as if you're wrapping a present.
2. Carefully cut out a full-page picture from a nature magazine.
3. Fold the picture in half, and in half again.
4. Cut it into four equal pieces.
5. Glue the picture onto the sides of the four juice boxes to make a puzzle. (You could double your fun and make it more challenging by doing both sides of the boxes with another picture.)
6. You might want to put clear contact paper over the picture to protect the puzzle, or tape the edges.

23

Sculpture

Symbols

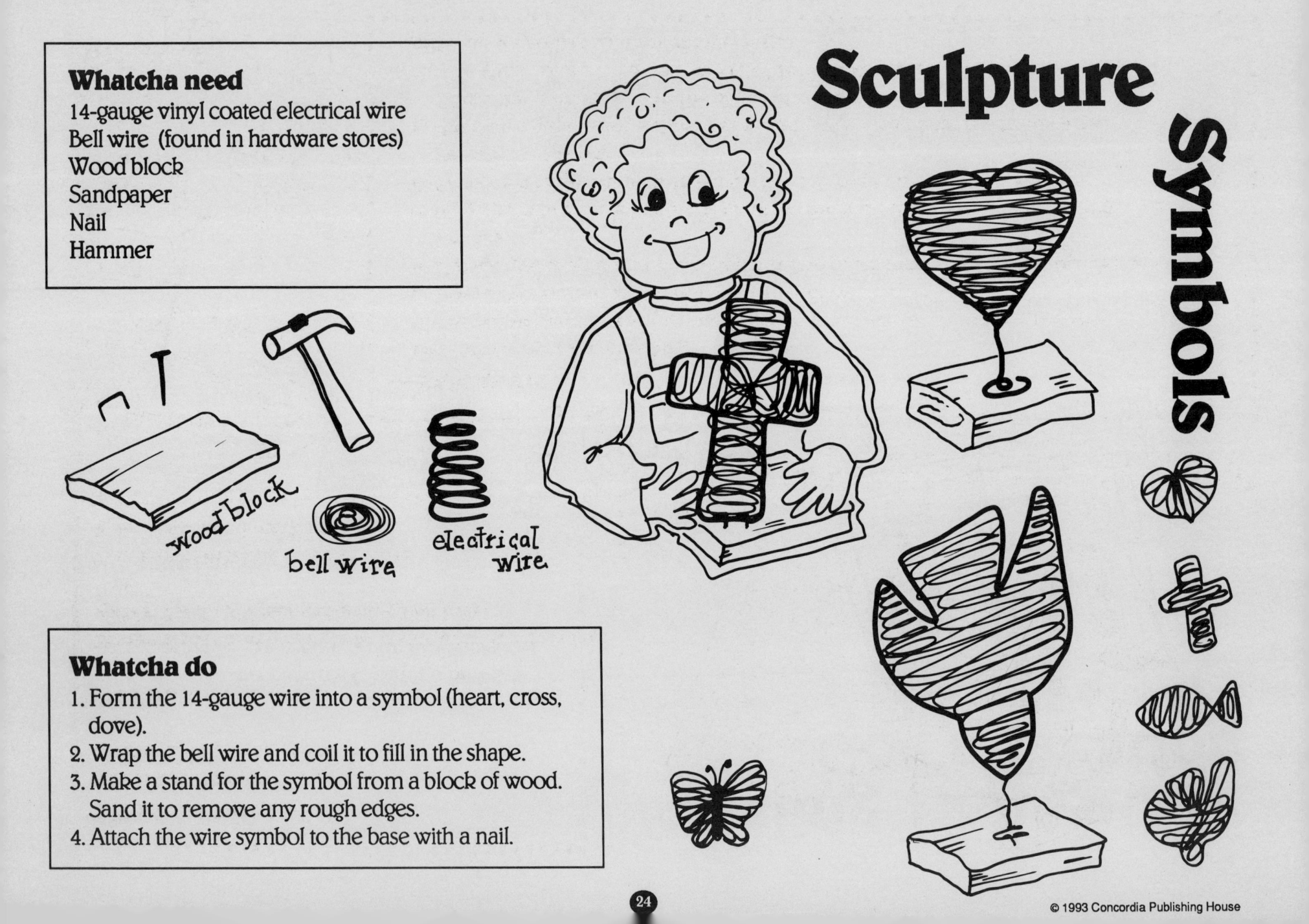

Whatcha need

14-gauge vinyl coated electrical wire
Bell wire (found in hardware stores)
Wood block
Sandpaper
Nail
Hammer

wood block

bell wire

electrical wire

Whatcha do

1. Form the 14-gauge wire into a symbol (heart, cross, dove).
2. Wrap the bell wire and coil it to fill in the shape.
3. Make a stand for the symbol from a block of wood. Sand it to remove any rough edges.
4. Attach the wire symbol to the base with a nail.

Whatcha need

White tissue paper
Rubber stamps and stamp pads
  or
Tempera paints and sponge shapes
  or
Tempera paints and objects to print (toilet tissue rolls, spools, forks, kitchen gadgets, small toys)
  or
Tempera paints and a shallow pan
Brightly colored markers

Wrapping Paper

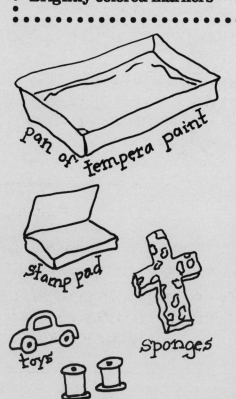

pan of tempera paint

stamp pad

toys

sponges

spools

Whatcha do

1. Lay tissue paper out on a large flat surface.
2. Choose from the following methods how to decorate the wrapping paper:
    a. Use rubber stamps and stamp pads to decorate tissue paper.
    b. Dip sponge shapes into tempera paint and print the shapes on the tissue paper. Let dry.
    c. Dip objects in tempera paint, then press them on the tissue paper. Let dry.
    d. Place each child's hand into tempera paint, then onto the tissue paper repeatedly. Let dry.
    e. Have each child place a thumb in a stamp pad, then onto the tissue paper. (Place the thumbprints in the shape of a heart or cross.)
3. Use brightly colored markers to write "Jesus loves (name of person receiving gift)" or any other appropriate messages.

Noah's Ark

Whatcha need

- One 12" x 18" piece of paper
- Crayons
- Blue watercolor wash (mix 1 tablespoon blue tempera powder in 1 cup water)
- Paintbrush
- One 8" paper plate
- Scissors
- Markers (*optional*)
- Animal pictures from nature magazines
- Poster board (*optional*)
- Glue

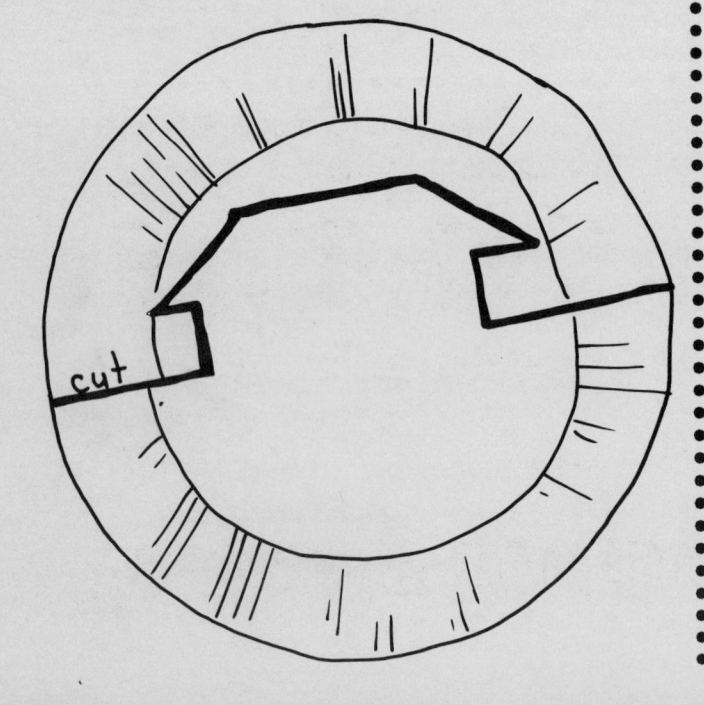

cut

Whatcha do

1. Color a scene of mountains, sky, trees, and clouds on the 12" x 18" paper. (Press hard when coloring so it shows through the watercolor wash later.)
2. Paint over the entire sheet with the blue watercolor wash. Let dry.
3. Cut the paper plate according to the ark pattern.
4. Use markers or crayons to decorate the back of the paper plate to look like an ark.
5. Cut animal pictures from magazines to put into the ark. If the animal pictures are too lightweight, glue them to poster board first, then cut them out.
6. Glue animals to the inside of the ark, facing out.
7. When the wash is dry, glue the ark onto the paper scene, back side up.

What's in the Egg?

Whatcha need

Construction paper
Scissors
Crayons or markers
Brad fasteners

Ducks

Birds

Dinosaurs

Fish

Snakes Turtles

Use this project to talk about God's creatures that hatch from eggs.

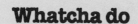

Whatcha do

1. Cut two egg shapes the same size from construction paper.
2. On the first egg shape, draw a picture of a baby animal that hatches from an egg.
3. Cut the second egg shape to look like it is a cracked egg shell.
4. Attach the cracked egg to the whole egg at the sides, using a brad fastener for each half egg. Now the egg can be "opened" to see what new life God sends to us.

Paper-Plate Puppet Stage

Whatcha need

One 8" paper plate
Fine-line markers
Scissors
Craft sticks

Whatcha do

1. Decorate the bottom half of the paper plate to be the ground (draw rocks, bushes, roads or paths).

2. Decorate the top half of the paper plate to be the sky (draw clouds and blue sky).

3. Cut a slit across the middle of the plate (about 4½—5" across) to separate the land and sky. You will insert each puppet through this slit from the back.

4. To make the puppets, draw a face and clothes on the top of the craft sticks. Leave room at the bottom of the sticks to hold the puppets.

Note: You may want to make two or three each of male and female puppets. These can be adapted to whatever Bible story is being presented.

Each child now has his or her own cast of characters and a puppet stage to tell a favorite Bible story to a friend or family member.

Butterfly Surprise

Whatcha need

One sheet white (or light-colored) construction paper

Tempera paints (black and three or four bright colors)

Squeeze bottles (plastic mustard or ketchup bottles)

The teacher will need to put the tempera paints into the squeeze bottles ahead of time.

fold

bottles of paint

drops of paint

Whatcha do

1. Fold the construction paper in half.
2. Draw half of a butterfly pattern onto the folded sheet of paper.
3. Cut out the butterfly. *Do not cut along the fold.*
4. Open the butterfly.
5. Drop black paint down the middle of the fold.
6. Drop different bright colors of paint sporadically on the right side of the butterfly.
7. Fold the left side of the butterfly over the right side and press down firmly. Rub to blend the colors.
8. Open and find your surprise!

Note: These butterflies can be hung on windows, from lights, on bulletin boards, or attached to a large banner to tell others about the new life Christ gives us.

CrissCross

Whatcha need
Typing paper
Crayons
Scissors
Colored construction paper
Glue

Whatcha do
1. Make texture rubbings from items in and around the church. (To make a texture rubbing, lay the typing paper over various textured surfaces. Each time, rub the crayon over the paper. The different texture will show on the typing paper.)
2. Cut a cross shape from the paper of texture rubbings.
3. Glue the cross onto the colored construction paper.

Variations: Cut a butterfly, heart, or fish shape from the texture-rubbing paper.

Christmas Pop-Up Card

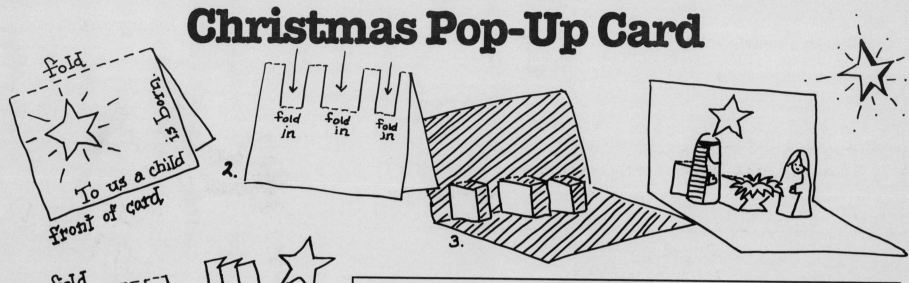

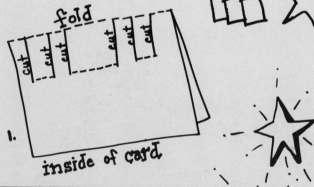

Whatcha need

Construction paper, various
  colors

Scissors

Collage materials

Glue

Markers

Whatcha do

1. Fold two same-size pieces of construction paper in half. Set one aside.
2. Cut the remaining piece according to the diagram.
3. Fold it back and forth along the fold line.
4. Set up the card like a tent. Push the three strips through to the other side of the card.
5. Close the card and press all folds firmly.
6. Open and see the strips pop up.
7. Using construction paper and collage materials, create Mary, Joseph, and Jesus in the manger.
8. Glue the figures to the three pop-up strips.
9. Accordion-fold a small strip, approximately 1½" long, three times. Glue a star on the end of the strip. Glue the other end on the card, above Jesus.
10. Decorate the other folded piece of paper as the front of the card.
11. Glue this to the pop-up card.

Getting to Know You

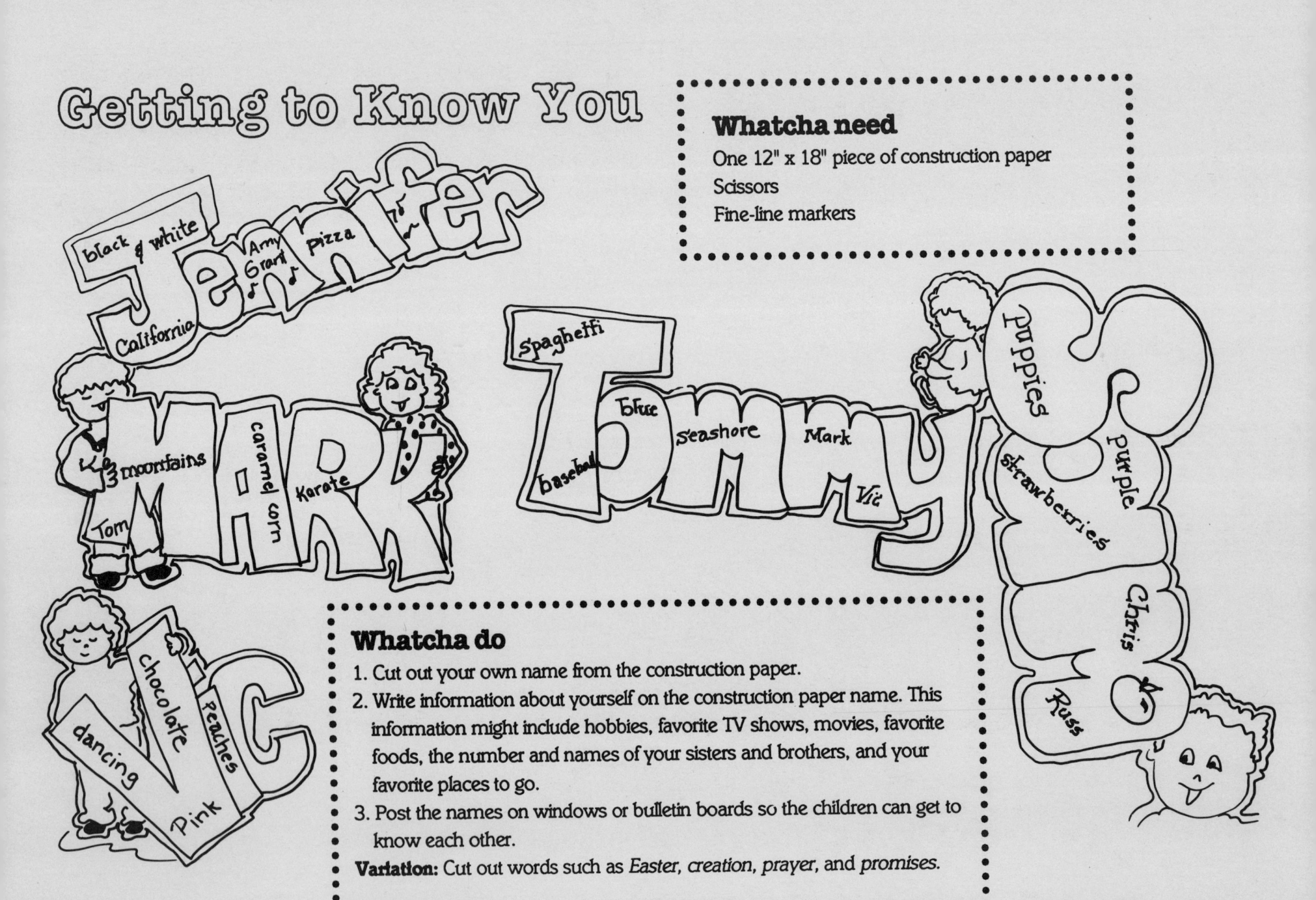

Whatcha need

One 12" x 18" piece of construction paper

Scissors

Fine-line markers

Whatcha do

1. Cut out your own name from the construction paper.
2. Write information about yourself on the construction paper name. This information might include hobbies, favorite TV shows, movies, favorite foods, the number and names of your sisters and brothers, and your favorite places to go.
3. Post the names on windows or bulletin boards so the children can get to know each other.

Variation: Cut out words such as *Easter, creation, prayer,* and *promises.*

Prayer Circle

Whatcha need

Plain paper
Scissors
Pencil
Fine-line markers

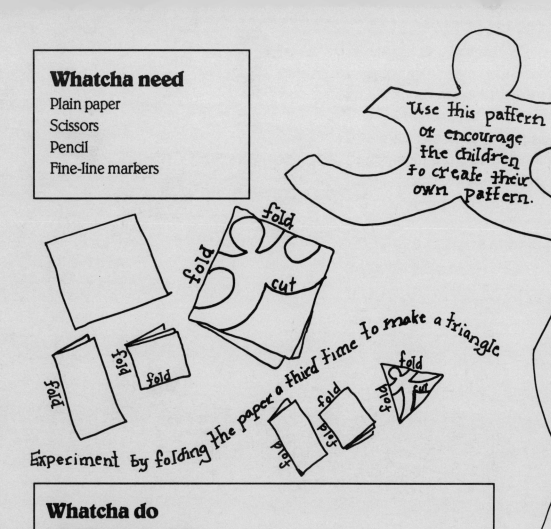

Use this pattern or encourage the children to create their own pattern.

fold

fold

fold

cut

fold

fold

fold

Experiment by folding the paper a third time to make a triangle

fold

fold

fold

cut

Whatcha do

1. Fold the paper in half.
2. Fold the paper in half again.
3. Cut off the rough-edge corner to round it.
4. Draw a paper doll shape with the head being in the folded corners.
5. Cut out the paper doll, being sure not to cut the folds at the hands. Unfold.
6. Write your prayer on the arms, which form a circle.

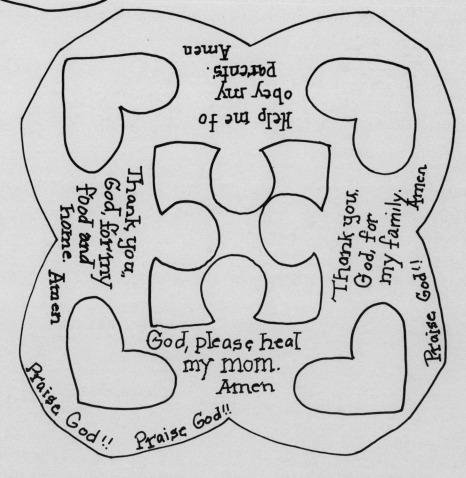

Thank you, God, for my food and home. Amen

Help me to obey my parents. Amen

Thank you, God, for my family. Amen

God, please heal my mom. Amen

Praise God!!

Praise God!!

Praise God!!

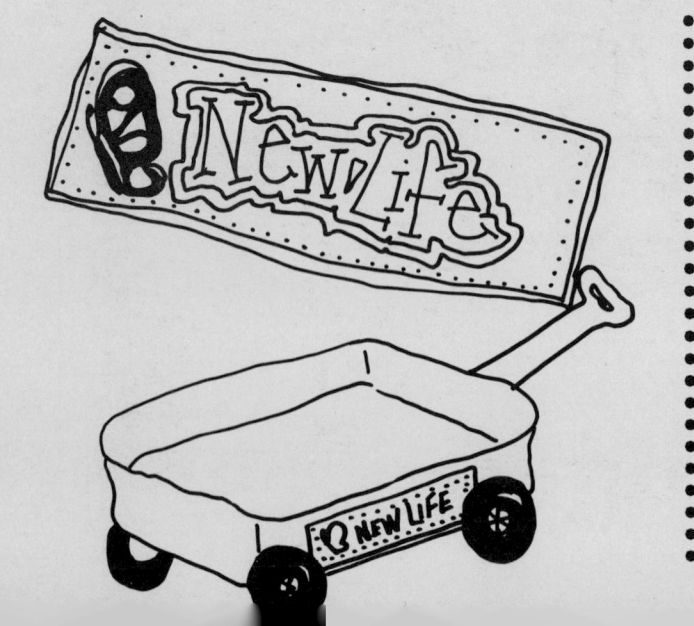

Whatcha need

Clear contact paper
Scissors
Paper, 4" x 12"
Pencils
Markers

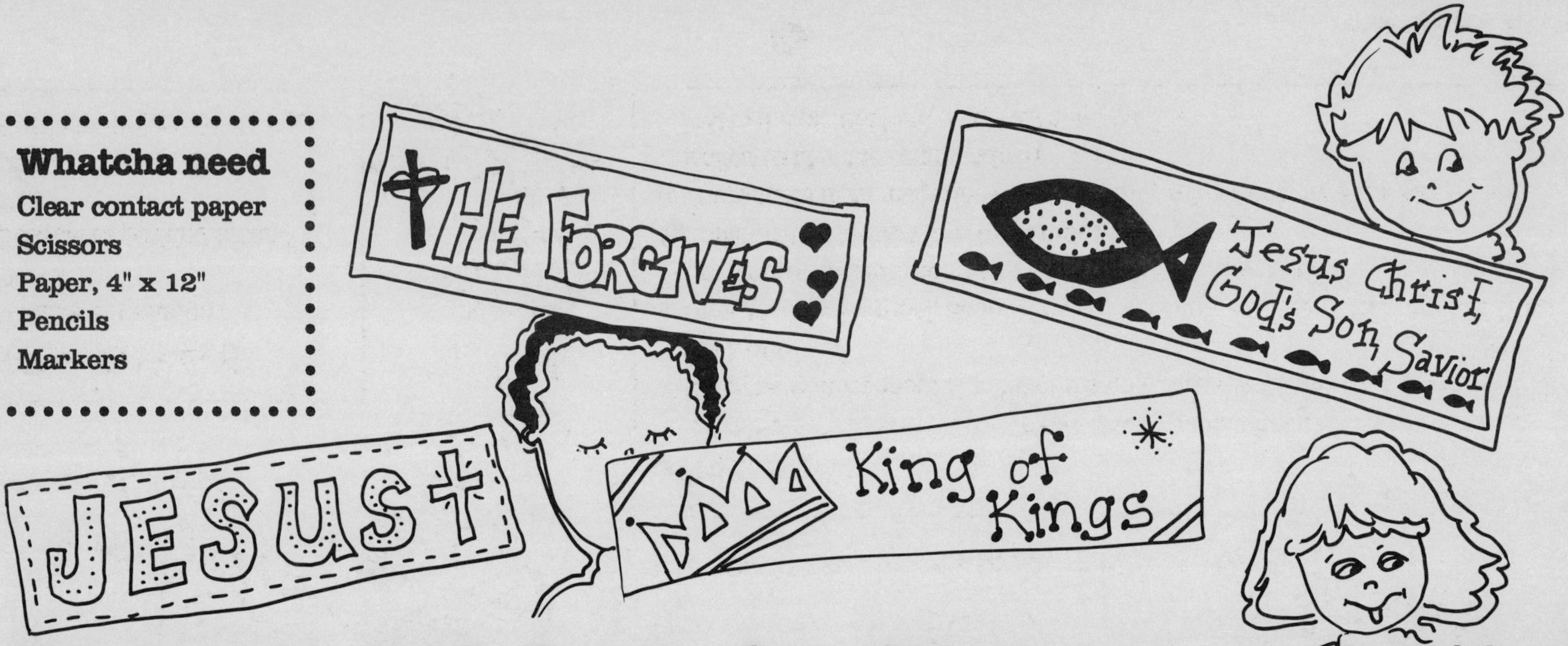
HE FORGIVES
Jesus Christ, God's Son, Savior
JESUS
King of Kings

Bumper Stickers for Wagons and Bikes

New Life
NEW LIFE

Whatcha do

1. Cut two pieces of contact paper. One should be 4" x 12" (to fit the back of the plain paper). One should be 5" x 13". This one will cover the front of the bumper sticker.
2. Write your message in one-inch-wide letters on the 4" x 12" paper.
3. Color in the background with dark markers, leaving the words white.
4. Decide where the bumper sticker is to be placed.
5. With the help of an adult, use the 5" x 13" piece of contact paper to adhere the bumper sticker.

Note: Be sure to ask parents' or grown-ups' permission to adhere the bumper sticker to objects.

Wallpaper Picture Frame

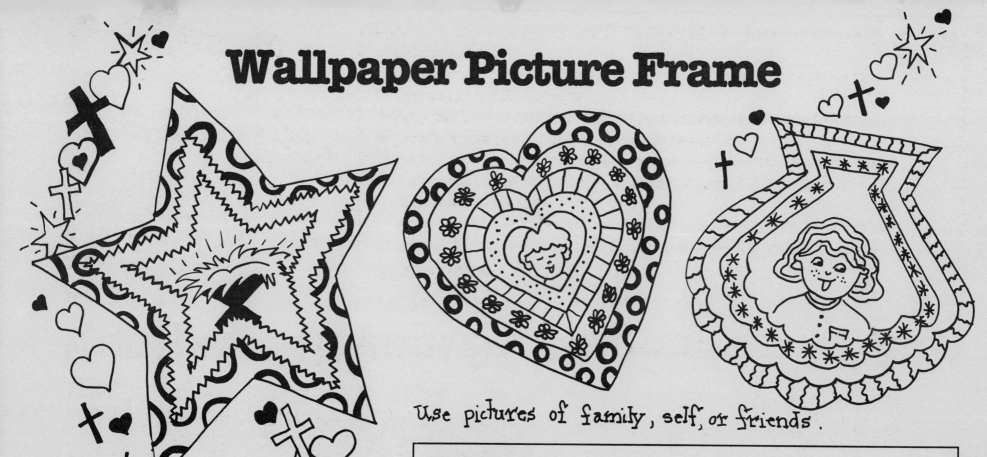

Use pictures of family, self, or friends.

Whatcha need

Wallpaper or fabric
Pencil
Scissors or pinking shears
Glue
Picture
Self-adhering picture hanger

Whatcha do

1. Choose a desired symbol (e.g., heart, cross, praying hands).
2. Draw the symbol about 3" in diameter on a piece of wallpaper or fabric.
3. Cut it out.
4. Draw the same symbol, about 1" bigger, on another piece of wallpaper or fabric. Cut it out; then glue the small one on top of the larger one.
5. Continue this process four to six times.
6. Cut pictures from magazines or old Sunday school and vacation Bible school leaflets to fit in the center; adhere.
7. Fasten the picture hanger to the center back.

35

Peanut Feet Puppet

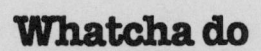

peanut candies

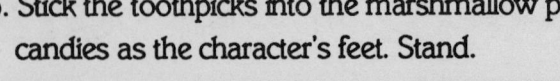

Whatcha need

Construction paper (various colors, perhaps fluorescent)

Markers or crayons

Scissors

Glue

Toothpicks

Marshmallow peanut candies

Whatcha do

1. Fold the paper in half.
2. Draw a 6" tall Bible character on one side.
3. Cut out the picture, using the folded paper so that you will have two identical characters.
4. Color in the features and clothes of your Bible character.
5. Glue the bodies together with the toothpicks coming out of the bottom as legs.
6. Stick the toothpicks into the marshmallow peanut candies, using the candies as the character's feet. Stand.

Paper Ba(g)sket

Whatcha need

- Brown or white paper lunch bag
- Scissors
- Crayons or markers

Keep the bag folded, cut only on the dotted lines.

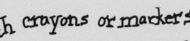 decorate the shapes with crayons or markers

cut

do not cut

Whatcha do

1. Cut off the top 4" of the bag. (Keep the cut-off section to use for the Paper Bag Wreath project on page 38.)
2. Laying the bag flat, draw the shape of a heart, cross, or butterfly onto the bag.
3. Cut away the top part from around the shape. See the diagram.
4. Color and decorate the shape on both sides of the bag.
5. Use as a gift bag or goody bag for a friend.

Paper Bag Wreath

Whatcha need

- Top 4" to 5" of the paper lunch bag left over from the Paper Ba(g)skets project
- Floral ribbon or gift ribbon
- Scissors
- Watercolor paper
- Hole punch

Hang hearts, bells, flowers, Baby Jesus, musical instruments, etc. from the center.

You may use two or three bag tops.

Crunch and twist the bag

Whatcha do

1. Open the top of the lunch bag so you have a circle.
2. Using both hands, crunch the paper together, moving your hands around the circle. When you're done, you'll have what looks like a wreath.
3. Cut the ribbon into 12"–18" lengths.
4. Tie a ribbon into a bow every 2" around the wreath.
5. You may want to curl the ends of the ribbons (if you've used curling ribbon), or just leave the ends flowing.
6. Cut a praying hand about 2" x 2" from the watercolor paper.
7. Punch a hole into the top of the praying hand.
8. Using ribbon, hang the praying hand from the top of the wreath so it hangs in the center of the wreath.

Note: The wreath reminds us of God's continuous love for us. The hand reminds us that God wants us to pray to Him continually (1 Thessalonians 5:17).

Circle Creation Banner

Whatcha need

- Six 8" paper plates or circles cut from colored paper
- Light- and dark-colored fabric or streamers
- Glue
- Blue and brown watercolors
- Paintbrush
- Objects from nature (rocks, sticks, leaves, shells)
- Fluorescent or metallic paper, aluminum foil, or star stickers
- Scissors
- Magazine
- Photo of yourself
- Crayons or markers (*optional*)
- Six 6" x 2" strips of paper or ribbon

Whatcha do

Day 1: Use half of the plate or circle for dark and half of the plate for light. Use light colored fabric or streamers for light, and dark fabric or streamers for dark.

Day 2: Use watercolors (blue and brown) to paint the earth and sky on the second paper plate.

Day 3: Glue objects from nature (that you have collected together or that students have brought from home) onto a third paper plate or circle.

Day 4: Cut stars out of metallic or fluorescent paper or from aluminum foil. Attach these or star stickers to a fourth plate to represent the stars, moon, and sun.

Day 5: Cut pictures of birds and fish from old magazines and glue these onto a fifth plate.

Day 6: Glue a photograph of yourself, your family, or the class onto a sixth plate or circle. You could also cut out pictures of animals and glue these (or draw them) on this page.
As each plate is completed, attach it below the previous plate, using the 6" paper strips, to make a long banner.

Stuffed Mobiles

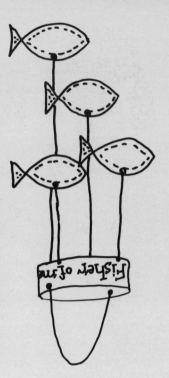

Fisher of me

Tom   Jill

Promises

Whatcha need

Construction paper
Markers
Scissors
Stapler
Cotton balls or tissues
Hole punch
Poster board, 18" x 2"
Yarn

Whatcha do

1. Choose a theme for the mobile.
2. Fold the construction paper in half.
3. Draw desired figures or symbols.
4. Use markers to decorate the shapes.
5. Cut out the shapes.
6. Staple ¾ of the sides of each of the shapes together.
7. Stuff the shape with cotton balls or tissue.
8. Staple the remainder of the shape closed.
9. Punch a hole in the top of each shape.
10. Write the theme or Bible verse on the strip of poster board.
11. Staple the poster board strip into a circle with the message showing on the outside.
12. Punch a hole along the bottom of the circle for each shape of the mobile. Tie each shape to the circle with a length of yarn.
13. Punch holes at the top of the circle; tie the yarn to each hole, then knot together these yarn strands as a hanger.

Praise Pop-Up Card

accordian fold one strip for each shape.

fold Celebrate

accordian fold behind each shape

Jesus love you

Encourage children to be creative with their shapes.

Whatcha need

Various colors of neon or
   fluorescent paper
Scissors
Construction paper strips (½" x
1½")
Glue
Foil confetti
Foil stars
Markers

Whatcha do

1. Cut out celebration shapes from the neon paper (stars, boys, girls, sunshines).
2. Accordion-fold the construction paper strips using one strip per shape.
3. Glue the shapes to the accordion folded strips; then glue the other end of the strip to one of the neon colored pieces of paper.
4. Glue confetti and foil stars around the card front and inside.
5. Use markers to write a Bible verse or praise words on the card.
6. Fold in half.
7. When you open the card, the shapes should spring out.

41

Cork Doorknob Hanger

Be patient God is not finished with me.

Hear & the Good News

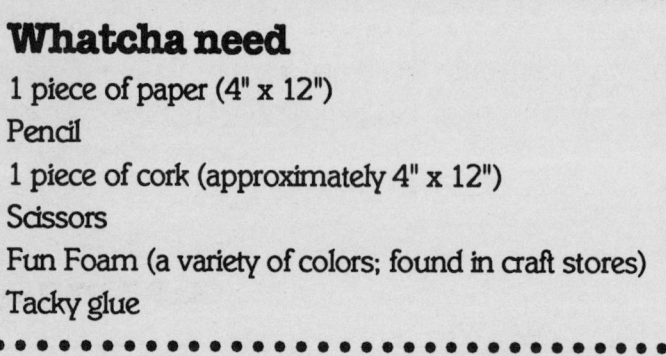

add jingle bells to the bottom

Prayer in progress

Whatcha do

1. Draw a design for the doorknob hanger on the piece of paper.
2. Cut a hole near the top of the cork for the doorknob to slip through.
3. Cut the Fun Foam and glue the shapes onto the cork according to your desired design. (It will take a while for the glued Fun Foam to dry.)

Fun Foam Heart Pockets

Whatcha need

Fun Foam
Scissors
Hole punch
Yarn or ribbon
Markers

Whatcha do

1. Cut a 6" heart from the Fun Foam.
2. Cut the bottom half of another 6" heart from a different color of Fun Foam.
3. Punch holes evenly around the heart.
4. Lay the heart over the half heart, mark the holes, and punch out the holes from the half-heart shape.
5. Place the half heart on the whole heart; use a ribbon or length of yarn to stitch the two pieces together (in and out of each hole).
6. Decorate with markers. Allow to dry before touching.

Note: Use the pockets for messages, prayer starters, Scripture memory verses, or place an invitation to vacation Bible school or Sunday school inside.

43

Fun Foam Magnets

Glue small pieces of foam to the shapes. Allow to dry overnight.

Fishers of Men

King of Kings

Whatcha do

1. Cut a symbol from the Fun Foam.
2. Cut additional pieces from other colors of Fun Foam to decorate your symbol. Glue these pieces on the symbol.
3. Adhere the magnetic strip to the back. You might want to write words on the symbols using markers.

Whatcha need

Clear acetate or stiff plastic
Scissors
Permanent markers (narrow tipped)
Hole punch

Encourage the children to try different shapes

Jesus ♥ me

Love Laces

Whatcha do

1. Cut two desired shapes (heart, cross, butterfly) from the acetate. Shapes should be about 2" x 2".
2. Use permanent markers to decorate the shapes with words of love for Jesus.
3. Punch two holes in each shape. The holes should be about ½" apart, and about ⅓ of the way from the top of the shape.
4. Place each shape over the bottom two holes of an unlaced shoe. Finish lacing the shoe.

Cotton Puff Creations

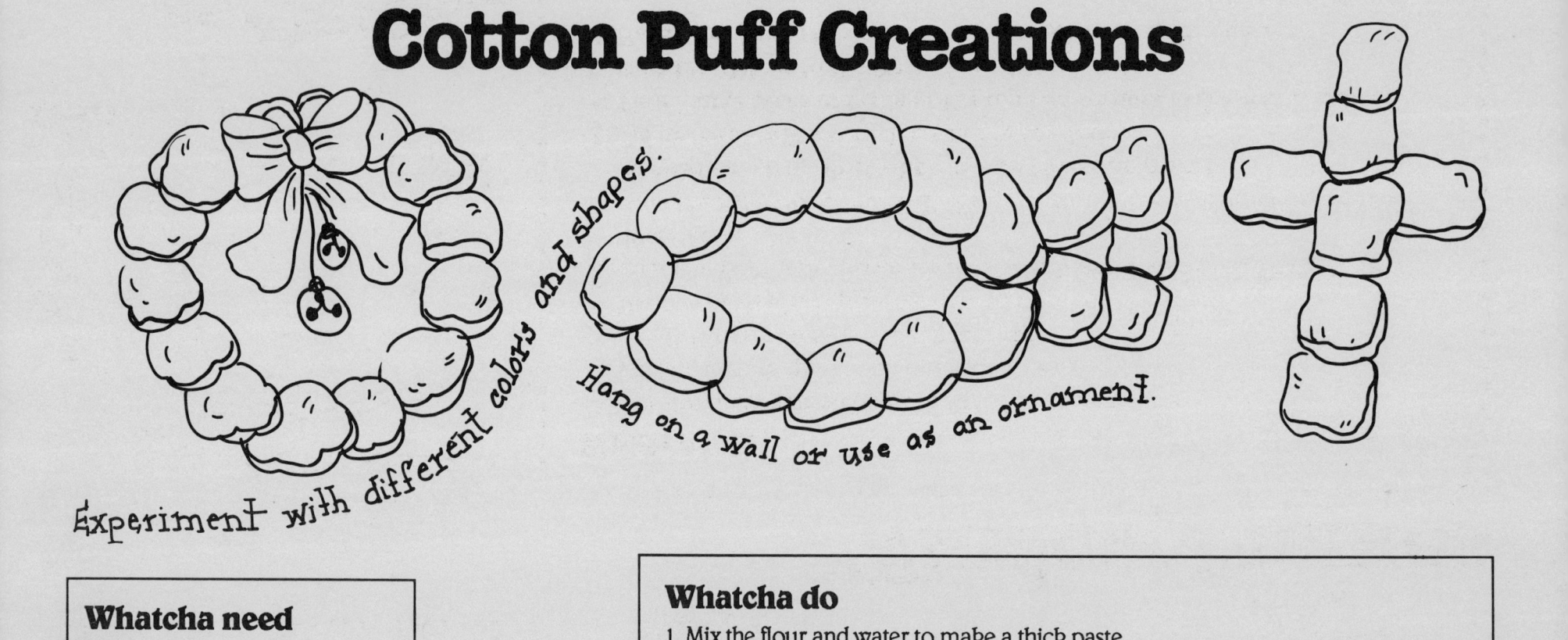

Experiment with different colors and shapes.

Hang on a wall or use as an ornament.

Whatcha need

Flour

Water

Bowl

Cotton balls

Waxed paper

Cookie sheet

Tempera paints

Paintbrushes

Clear acrylic spray

Food coloring (optional)

Whatcha do

1. Mix the flour and water to make a thick paste.
2. Dip the cotton balls into the paste.
3. Arrange the dipped cotton balls on a waxed paper-covered cookie sheet in a desired shape. The cotton balls need to touch each other.
4. Let dry overnight.
5. Paint with tempera paint; allow it to dry.
6. Spray with acrylic spray. **(Adults need to do this in a well-ventilated area, away from children.)**
7. Peel off the waxed paper.

Variation: Add food coloring or tempera paint to the paste before dipping the cotton balls.

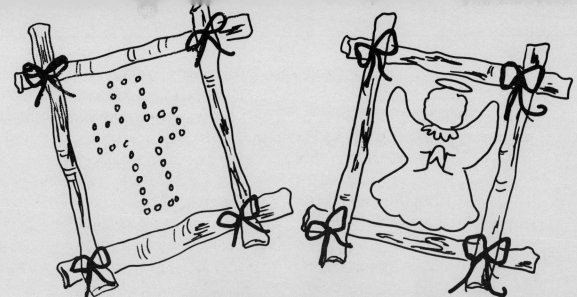

Window Frames

Whatcha need

- Construction paper
- Scissors
- Pencil
- Styrofoam meat tray
- Push pin
- Twigs
- Glue gun
- Raffia

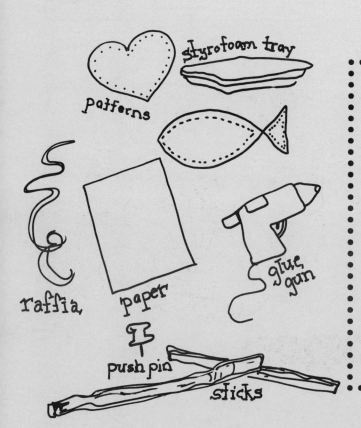

patterns

styrofoam tray

raffia

paper

push pin

glue gun

sticks

Whatcha do

1. Cut the construction paper into a 3" x 4" rectangle.
2. Draw a simple symbol on one side.
3. Lay the paper on top of the meat tray.
4. Use the push pin to puncture holes around the symbol.
5. To make the frame, break or cut the twigs into two 4-inch and two 5-inch pieces.
6. Glue the twigs together with the glue gun to form a frame with a 3" x 4" opening. **(An adult should use the glue gun.)**
7. Tie pieces of raffia at each corner of the frame.
8. Tie a longer piece of raffia at the top two corners to serve as a hanger.
9. Glue the picture to the frame from the back side.
10. Hang the picture in a window where light shines through.

Yarn Symbols

Whatcha need

Plain paper
Pencil
Waxed paper
Glue
Bowl
Heavy yarn
Scissors
Colored cellophane (*optional*)

patterns

glue.

yarn

waxed paper

Whatcha do

1. Draw a symbol on the paper.
2. Cover the picture with waxed paper.
3. Pour the glue into the bowl.
4. Pull the yarn through the bowl of glue.
5. Outline the drawing with the glue-coated yarn. All lines must touch or cross over each other.
6. Let dry overnight.
7. Peel off the waxed paper and hang the picture from a light or window.

Option: Cut a piece of colored cellophane to fit the shape and glue it to the back of the symbol.

Wooden Plaque

Whatcha need

- Wood (scrap wood in appropriate sizes for plaques)
- Sandpaper
- Permanent markers, colored glue, acrylic paint, or puff paint
- Black or brown paste shoe polish (do not use liquid)
- Soft cloth
- Clear acrylic spray

colored glue, or paint

paste shoe polish

Wood

Sand paper

Whatcha do

1. Sand the rough edges on the wood until smooth.
2. Use markers, paint, or colored glue to decorate the plaque. Let dry overnight.
3. Rub a small amount of black or brown shoe polish over the plaque; buff with a soft cloth.
4. Spray the plaque with acrylic spray. **(An adult should spray in a well-ventilated area, away from children.)**
5. Adhere the picture hanger to the center back of the plaque.

49

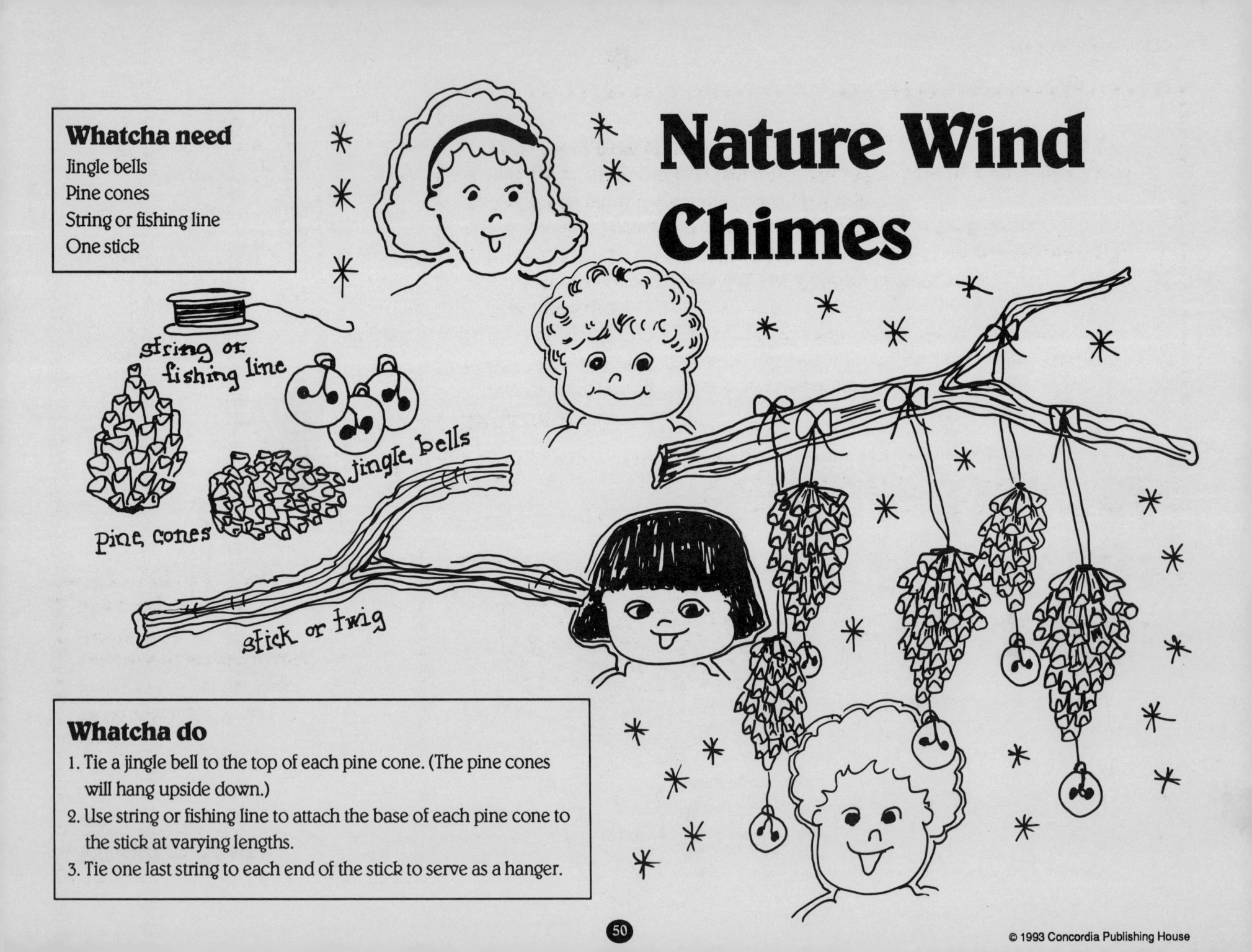

Nature Wind Chimes

Whatcha need

Jingle bells
Pine cones
String or fishing line
One stick

string or fishing line

pine cones

jingle bells

stick or twig

Whatcha do

1. Tie a jingle bell to the top of each pine cone. (The pine cones will hang upside down.)
2. Use string or fishing line to attach the base of each pine cone to the stick at varying lengths.
3. Tie one last string to each end of the stick to serve as a hanger.

Mix the dough thoroughly.

water

paints

Acrylic Spray

candle

Foil

Flour

ziplock bag

salt

Candle Holders

Whatcha do

1. Pour 1 cup flour and ½ cup salt into a ziplock bag and mix.
2. Add ⅓ cup water to the bag, make sure all the air is out, and reseal.
3. Use your hands around the outside of the bag to work the dough. Mix thoroughly.
4. Take the dough out of the bag and form a desired shape.
5. Press the candle into the shape to form a holder. Then remove the candle.
6. Bake on a foil-covered cookie sheet at 225 degrees for 2 hours.
7. Cool. Then paint the candle holder. Let dry.
8. Spray with acrylic spray. (An adult should do this in a well-ventilated area, away from children.)

Wooden Planter

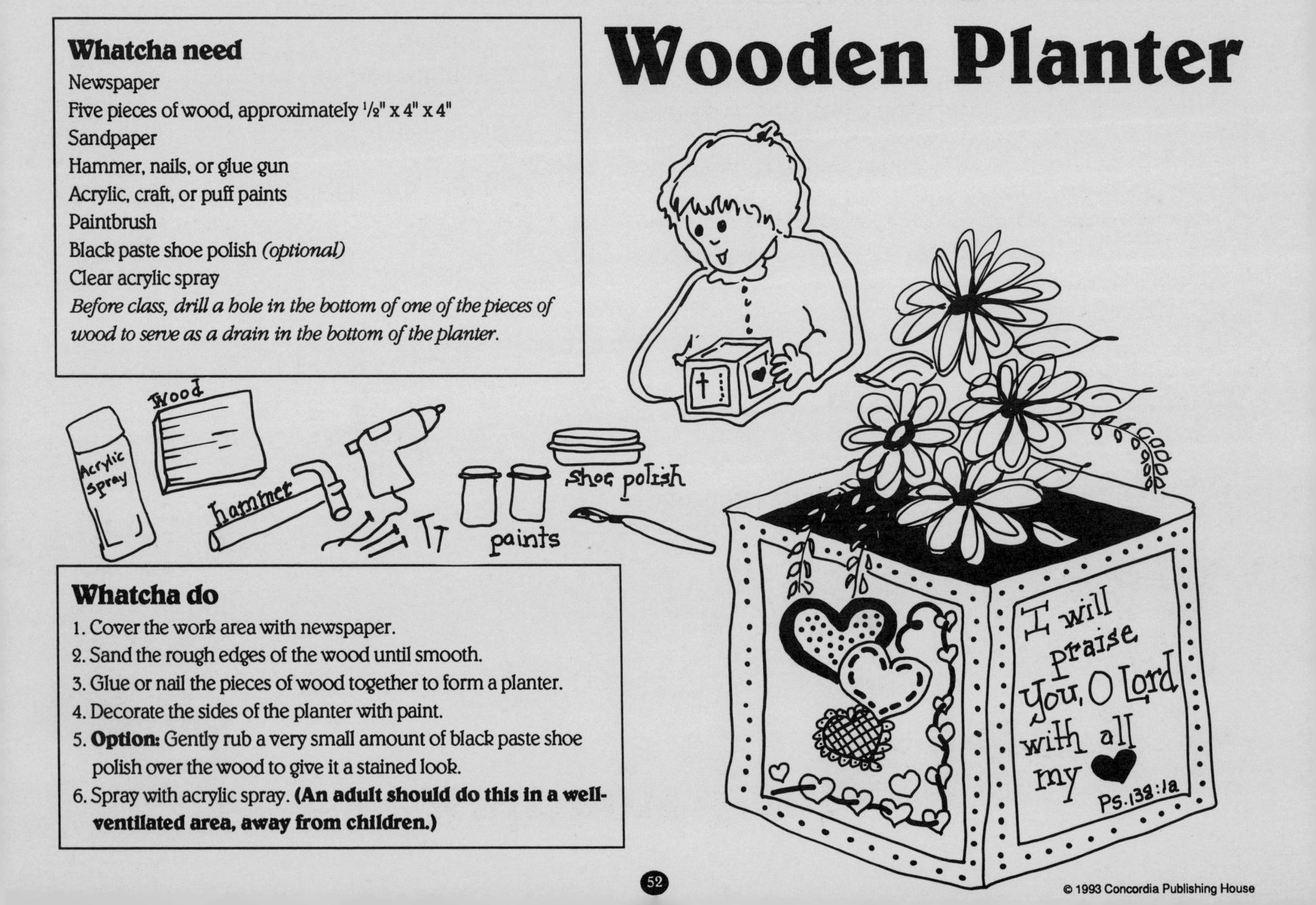

Whatcha need

Newspaper

Five pieces of wood, approximately ½" x 4" x 4"

Sandpaper

Hammer, nails, or glue gun

Acrylic, craft, or puff paints

Paintbrush

Black paste shoe polish *(optional)*

Clear acrylic spray

Before class, drill a hole in the bottom of one of the pieces of wood to serve as a drain in the bottom of the planter.

Whatcha do

1. Cover the work area with newspaper.
2. Sand the rough edges of the wood until smooth.
3. Glue or nail the pieces of wood together to form a planter.
4. Decorate the sides of the planter with paint.
5. **Option:** Gently rub a very small amount of black paste shoe polish over the wood to give it a stained look.
6. Spray with acrylic spray. **(An adult should do this in a well-ventilated area, away from children.)**

I will praise you, O Lord with all my ♥ Ps. 138:1a

Rainbow Pasta

Whatcha need

Food coloring: red, orange, yellow, green, blue

Rubbing alcohol

Ziplock bag or a bowl

A variety of shapes and sizes of pasta, including rigatoni

Newspaper

Shoelaces

Poster board

Christian symbols (see patterns)

Glue

Whatcha do

1. Combine 2 teaspoons food coloring and ½ cup rubbing alcohol in a ziplock bag or a bowl.
2. Add 2 cups of the pasta and mix.
3. Pour the pasta onto newspaper to dry.
4. Repeat this procedure with each color.
5. Use the shoelace to string the rigatoni into a necklace.
6. Cut Christian symbols from poster board. Glue pasta in a pattern on the symbols.

Fabric Cross

Whatcha do

1. Mix equal parts of glue and water in a mixing bowl.
2. Soak the fabric in the glue mixture.
3. Squeeze out the excess glue from the fabric.
4. Smooth out the fabric and hang to dry overnight. (Place newspaper under the fabric to catch the glue that drips.)
5. When dry, iron the fabric.
6. Use a scissors or pinking shears to cut 1" x 4" strips of fabric.
7. Fold each strip over and staple.
8. Use glue or staples to adhere the fabric strips to the cross. See the diagram.
9. Glue a large decorative button to the center.
10. Adhere the picture hanger to the center top of the back of the cross.

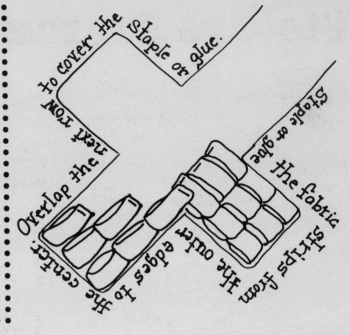

Staple at glue.
Overlap the next row to cover the staple or glue.
Overlap the fabric strips from the outer edges to the center.

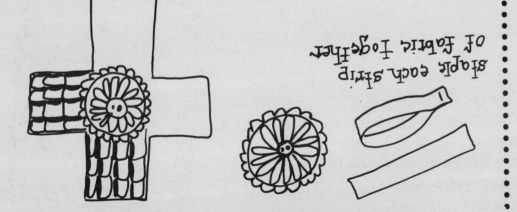

Staple each strip of fabric together.

Picture Frame

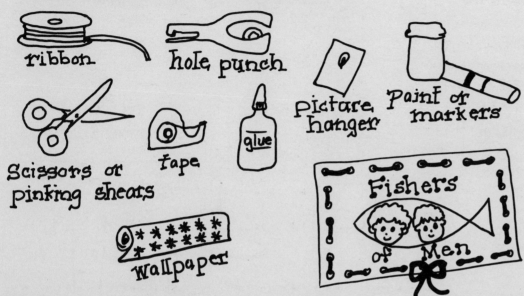

ribbon

hole punch

picture hanger

Paint or markers

glue

Scissors or pinking shears

tape

Wallpaper

Fishers of Men

Whatcha need

- 2 wallpaper pieces, 8" x 10"
- Scissors or pinking shears
- Photo of yourself or your family
- Tape
- Glue
- Hole Punch
- Ribbon
- Self-adhesive picture hanger
- Craft paint (*optional*)

Jesus me!

Whatcha do

1. Cut a shape from the center of one piece of wallpaper.
2. Tape the photo to the back of the opening.
3. Glue the second piece of wallpaper to the back of the photo.
4. Use the hole punch to evenly punch holes around the frame.
5. Weave the ribbon through the holes, tying a bow at the top or bottom.
6. Attach the picture hanger to the back.

Optional: Use craft paint to write "Jesus loves me" on the front of the frame.

Accordion Picture Frame

wall paper

photos

scissors

craft glue

ribbons

rickrack

washers

 buttons

 seeds

Whatcha need

Wallpaper (12" x 18")

Scissors

Pictures or photos

Craft glue

Decorations for the frame, such
   as ribbon, rickrack, seeds,
   twigs, washers, buttons, silk
   flowers *(optional)*

Whatcha do

1. Cut the wallpaper into two 6" x 18" pieces.
2. Accordion-fold both pieces of wallpaper into four equal sections.
3. Carefully cut a shape from each section of one piece of the
   wallpaper.
4. Glue favorite pictures or photos behind each cut-out section.
5. Glue the remaining piece of paper to the back of the pictures.
6. Decorate the frame with ribbon, rickrack, tiny pearls, flowers, or
   items of your choice that you may have in your craft supply.

Make-a-Joyful-Noise Wind Chimes

Whatcha need

- Large wooden bead
- Jute twine
- Clay flower pot (3" or 4" in diameter)
- Items to hang, such as sea shells, old spoons, wooden craft sticks, wooden ice cream spoons
- String
- Scissors
- Craft glue or glue gun
- Craft paint or markers
- Clear acrylic spray

Try pieces of bamboo or strips of clear acrylic.

Pull the twine through the bead. Knot at the bottom.

Jesus ♥ me

Whatcha do

1. String the wooden bead onto the jute twine; tie to make a circle.
2. Pull the twine through the hole in the flower pot. The bead should be on the inside. The loop above the bottom of the pot becomes the hanger.
3. Using craft glue or a glue gun, adhere 6" to 8" lengths of string to the items you've chosen to hang. Let dry.
4. Remember to turn the flower pot upside down, then decorate it by using paint markers or craft paint. Spray with acrylic spray. (An adult should do this in a well-ventilated area, away from children.)
5. Glue the other end of the strings (on the hanging items) to the inside edge of the flower pot.

57

Bead Wind Chimes

Whatcha need

Dough (four or five colors)
Powder tempera or food coloring
Ziplock bag
Toothpicks
Foil-covered cookie sheet
Clear acrylic spray
Newspaper
Yarn or jute twine
Sturdy stick

Jute or yarn

Toothpicks

Acrylic Spray

mix several colors of dough

bake beads

God

Jesus

Savior

Friend

Son of God

Whatcha do

1. Make your dough: Mix 1 cup flour, ¼ cup salt, and 2 tablespoons powdered tempera paint; add ¼ to ½ cup water. If sticky, add more flour; if dry, add more water. Mix the dough well. Then set it aside in a ziplock bag and repeat the recipe until all the colors are made.
   To use food coloring to color the dough, add a few drops to the water, then mix into other ingredients.
2. Roll a variety of shapes and colors of beads. Use a toothpick to poke a hole in each bead.
3. Bake beads at 250 degrees for one hour on a foil-covered cookie sheet.
4. Place cooled beads on newspaper and spray with acrylic spray. **(An adult should do this in a well-ventilated area, away from children.)** Let dry.
5. String the beads, tying a knot between each bead to keep the beads in place.
6. Tie three or four strings of beads to a sturdy stick.

Stained-Glass Suncatchers

Whatcha need

- Dough (see recipe for Bead Wind Chimes on page 58)
- Rolling pin
- Cookie cutters or plastic knife
- Foil-covered cookie sheet
- Pencil
- Hard candies (a variety of colors)
- Small ziplock bags, one for each color
- Hammer or rubber mallet
- Newspaper
- Clear acrylic spray
- Yarn or ribbon

Whatcha do

1. Roll dough to ¼" thickness.
2. Use cookie cutters or a plastic knife to cut desired shapes.
3. Place shapes on foil-covered cookie sheet.
4. Use a plastic knife to carefully cut openings in the shapes.
5. Use a pencil to make a hole at the top of each shape.
6. Bake at 225 degrees for 15 minutes; remove from oven, but leave on the cookie sheet. Cool. Set oven to 375 degrees.
7. Place each color of candy in separate bags. Use the hammer or mallet to crush the candies.
8. Fill the openings of the shapes with the candies, using one color per opening.
9. Bake at 375 degrees for 8–10 minutes, or until the candy has melted.
10. Cool; remove from the cookie sheet and place the suncatchers on newspaper.
11. Spray with acrylic spray. (**An adult needs to do this in a well-ventilated area, away from children.**)
12. String a length of ribbon or yarn through the top hole and hang in a window or near a light.

Variation: Roll the dough into coils and form the shapes, making sure all the coils touch.

Whatcha need

- Scraps of paper (construction paper, watercolor paper, art paper, white typing paper)
- Blender
- Water
- Tub
- Clean, stretched screen
- Large sponge
- Matte board (found in craft stores)
- Acid-free double-stick tape (found in craft and art supply stores)
- Permanent marker (*optional*)
- Stick (*optional*)
- Curling ribbon (*optional*)

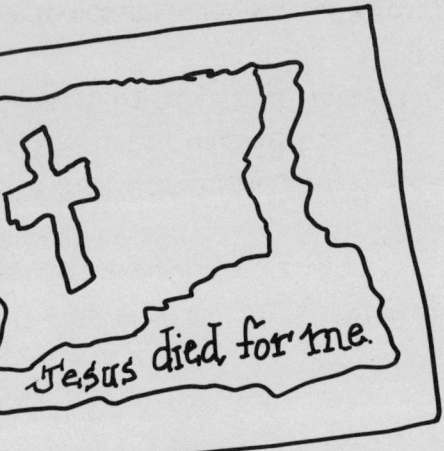

Jesus died for me.

Homemade Paper

Pour the liquid onto a screen. Use a sponge to press out the excess water. Let dry.

Whatcha do

1. Tear the paper into 1" strips; soak these in water approximately 15 minutes.
2. Be careful not to overwork your blender. Put about ½ cup of paper into the blender, fill with water, and blend for one minute.
3. Pour the mixture into the tub; repeat step 2 several times.
4. Over a sink or working outdoors, slowly pour the mixture from the tub over the clean screen.
5. Carefully press out excess water with the sponge.
6. Let dry overnight.
7. Carefully peel the paper from the screen.
8. Secure the paper shape to the matte board with tape.

Variations: Use a permanent marker to write a Bible verse on the paper. Add a stick and curling ribbon to make a flower. See the diagram. Or overlap several pieces to create a picture.

pattern

Suncatchers

Whatcha need

- Food coloring in several colors
- One 4-ounce bottle of glue per color
- Paper
- Pencil
- Clear plastic plates or lids
- Black fabric paint in squeeze applicator
- Hole punch
- Yarn or ribbon

Whatcha do

1. Mix the food coloring with the glue using these ratios:

Red:	20 drops	Orange:	6 red drops + 14 yellow drops
Blue:	20 drops	Teal:	15 blue drops + 5 green drops
Green:	20 drops	Purple:	14 red drops + 6 blue drops
Yellow:	20 drops		

   Let colored glue set overnight.

2. Draw a design on a piece of paper the same size as the plate or lid.

3. Place the plate over the design; use the black fabric paint to "draw" the design on the plate. Allow to dry overnight.

4. Carefully fill in the open spaces with the colored glue, using one color per space. (Pop any air bubbles with a pin.) Allow to dry overnight.

5. Punch a hole in the top of the plate; string a length of ribbon or yarn to serve as a hanger and tie in a knot.

6. Hang your suncatcher in a window to catch God's rays of sunlight.

Painted Flower Pot Ornaments

Whatcha do

1. Use the paint markers to decorate the flower pot. Be sure you hold the flower pot upside down as you make your design.
2. Outline the designs with a black paint marker.
3. Make a knotted loop with the jute twine.
4. String the bead; then make a knot at the bottom of the jute.
5. Tie a knot about halfway up the loop and pull through the hole in the bottom of the flower pot to create a hanger.

Witness Flower Pots

Whatcha need

Fabric (a variety of colors and small prints)

Scissors

Glue

Water

Bowl

Small flower pot (4" – 5" diameter)

Black fabric paint in squeezable applicator

Whatcha do

1. Cut Christian symbols from the fabric.
2. Dip the fabric symbols into equal parts of glue and water. Squeeze out the excess glue.
3. Arrange the symbols on the flower pot. Allow to dry.
4. Outline the fabric shapes with the black fabric paint. This will cover the edges of the fabric and make the designs stand out.

Vinyl Mosaic

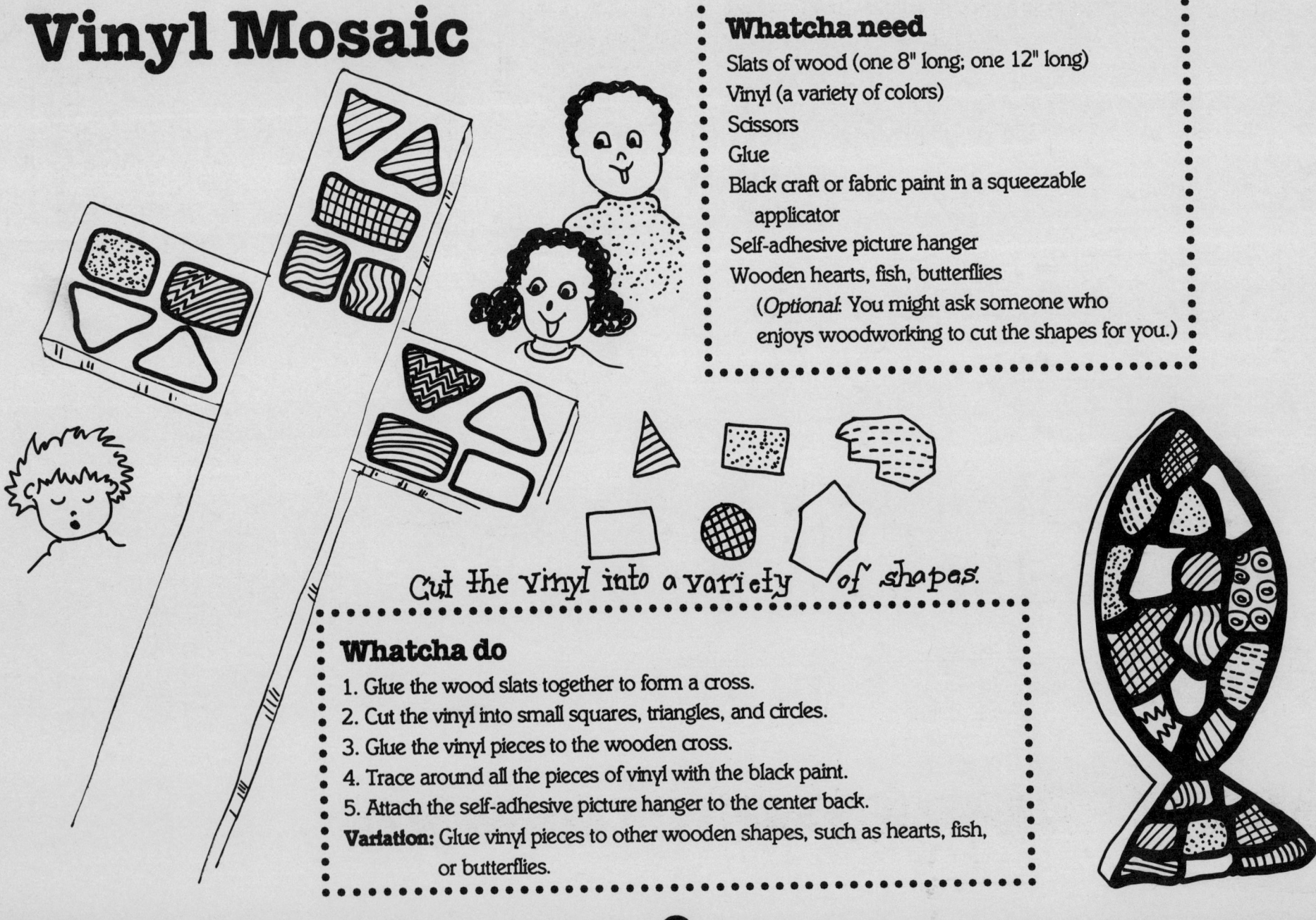

Whatcha need

Slats of wood (one 8" long; one 12" long)

Vinyl (a variety of colors)

Scissors

Glue

Black craft or fabric paint in a squeezable
   applicator

Self-adhesive picture hanger

Wooden hearts, fish, butterflies
   (*Optional:* You might ask someone who
      enjoys woodworking to cut the shapes for you.)

Cut the vinyl into a variety of shapes.

Whatcha do

1. Glue the wood slats together to form a cross.
2. Cut the vinyl into small squares, triangles, and circles.
3. Glue the vinyl pieces to the wooden cross.
4. Trace around all the pieces of vinyl with the black paint.
5. Attach the self-adhesive picture hanger to the center back.

Variation: Glue vinyl pieces to other wooden shapes, such as hearts, fish,
   or butterflies.

Stand-Up Bible Story

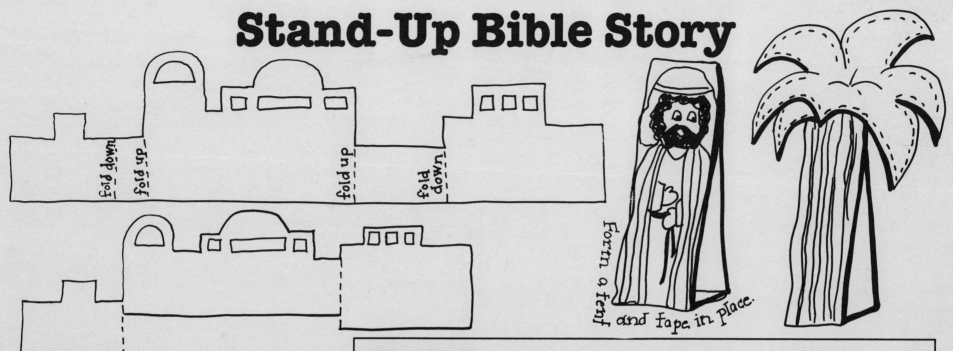

fold down

fold up

fold up

fold down

Form a tent and tape in place.

Whatcha do

1. Draw a Biblical city skyline on a piece of construction paper about 18" x 6".
2. Cut out the skyline.
3. Fold according to the diagram. The skyline will then be two-dimensional and it will stand up.
4. To make puppets, cut strips of construction paper for each character in the Bible story (approximately 1" x 10").
5. Fold each strip in half. About ½" to ¾" from the bottom, fold again to form the base.
6. Draw Bible characters' faces and clothing on the folded strips of paper, using both the front and the back.
7. Refold the bottom to form a tent shape. Tape in place.

Note: Use the puppets and the city scene to tell or retell a Bible story. For "Jesus Feeds 5,000" use a landscape that includes trees and bushes.

Whatcha need

Construction paper
Pencil
Scissors
Markers
Tape
Fabric scraps *(optional)*

Nonedible Creations

Whatcha need

Cereal (Grape Nuts or Shredded Wheat)
Glue
Bowl
Waxed paper
Clear acrylic spray
Self-adhesive picture hanger
Tempera paint and paintbrush (*optional*)

Cereal

Glue

Acrylic Spray

Paint

Whatcha do

1. Mix cereal with glue in a small bowl. Cereal should be covered with glue, but not runny.
2. Form the desired shape on waxed paper. Allow to dry for two to three days.
3. Spray the creation with acrylic spray. **(An adult should do this step in a ventilated area, away from children.)**
4. Attach the picture hanger on the center back.
Option: Paint the creation with tempera paint. Let dry. Then spray it with acrylic.

Make sure children understand

These are not cookies.

Bottle of Waves

Glue the caps on the bottles.

oil

water

Remove the base.

waves

Crayon
Crayon

blue food coloring

Water

Add shavings of crayons to water.

Whatcha need

One plastic 2-liter soda bottle
Water
Cooking oil or mineral oil
Blue food coloring
Crayon shavings *(optional)*

Whatcha do

1. Remove the bottom cover from the plastic 2-liter bottle.
2. Fill the bottle 3/4 full of water. Add several drops of blue food coloring, then fill to the top with oil. Pour the oil into the water slowly.
3. Close tightly.
4. Hold the bottle horizontally and tip the bottle from side to side.

Variation: Fill the bottle 7/8 full of water. Add crayon shavings and close tightly. Turn the bottle upside down and watch the colors "dance."

GROUP ACTIVITIES

"Jesus Feeds 5,000" Cut and Tell

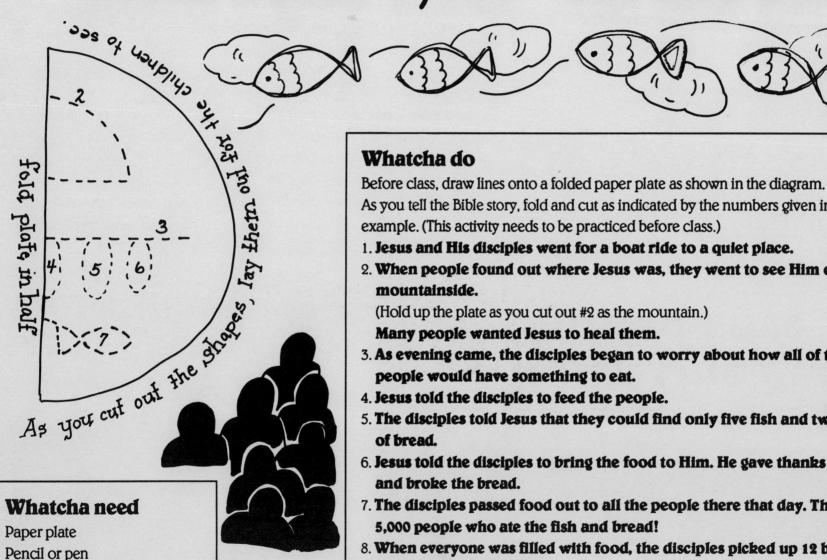

As you cut out the shapes, lay them out for the children to see.

fold plate in half

Whatcha do

Before class, draw lines onto a folded paper plate as shown in the diagram.

As you tell the Bible story, fold and cut as indicated by the numbers given in the story example. (This activity needs to be practiced before class.)

1. **Jesus and His disciples went for a boat ride to a quiet place.**
2. **When people found out where Jesus was, they went to see Him on the mountainside.**

    (Hold up the plate as you cut out #2 as the mountain.)

    Many people wanted Jesus to heal them.
3. **As evening came, the disciples began to worry about how all of these people would have something to eat.**
4. **Jesus told the disciples to feed the people.**
5. **The disciples told Jesus that they could find only five fish and two loaves of bread.**
6. **Jesus told the disciples to bring the food to Him. He gave thanks to God and broke the bread.**
7. **The disciples passed food out to all the people there that day. There were 5,000 people who ate the fish and bread!**
8. **When everyone was filled with food, the disciples picked up 12 baskets of food that were left over!**

Whatcha need

Paper plate
Pencil or pen
Scissors

Whatcha need

Silhouette of Jesus
Glue, tape, or stapler
Many red construction paper squares, about 4" x 4"
Scissors
Pencils

If Just One Person Showed Love

Whatcha do

1. Cut out a silhouette of Jesus from a large piece of table paper or black construction paper.

2. Attach the Jesus figure to a bulletin board, wall space, or door, and add the words, "If just one person showed love . . ." above or to the side.

3. Have the red construction-paper squares available for the students' use. Each time a child "shows love" to another student (forgives someone, lets someone go first in line, gives a compliment, shares), he or she takes a red square and cuts it into the shape of a heart. Then the child will write down the incident of showing love onto the heart and attach it onto or around the silhouette of Jesus.

4. Sit back and see how anxious students are to be kind, courteous, and forgiving. Eventually showing love becomes a wonderful habit!

Wallpaper 'Toons

The Good Samaritan

The Robbers

The Priest

The Levite

The Samaritan

The Inn

Whatcha need

Wallpaper books
Scissors
Glue
Tape

wallpaper books

Glue

Scissors

Tape

Whatcha do

1. As a group, choose a Bible story.
2. Choose four to five scenes from the story. Children may work on each page as individuals or in groups of two or three.
3. Choose the appropriate number of wallpaper pages to be the background of each scene.
4. Cut shapes out of the wallpaper to make the scenes (homes, trees, roads, people).
5. Glue the shapes onto the background paper.
6. Have a representative from each group tell what is happening in their scene.
7. The scenes can be taped together or put on a bulletin board to tell the story in correct sequence.

Nativity Skirt

Whatcha need

Butcher paper
Crayons, markers, or paints
Scissors
Construction paper
Glue
Poster board

Whatcha do

1. Divide the class into two groups.
2. Group 1 will measure a piece of butcher paper long enough to go around half the Christmas tree, or the length of a table or piano top, by 12" high.
3. Using markers, crayons, or paint, the group will draw and color a background representing the little town of Bethlehem.
4. Group 2 will draw and cut out 8" figures to be used in the nativity scene (Mary, Joseph, shepherds), or 3"–4" figures for the manger (sheep and cattle).
5. Cut out a 3" triangle for each character (smaller for the 4" figures).
6. Fold ½" of one side of the triangle over.
7. Glue this section to the back of the character to provide a stand.
8. Stand the background up around the tree. (You may need to support the background by connecting it to the tree or by gluing strips of poster board in several places to help it stand.)
9. Place the characters in front of the scenery, or tape or glue the characters directly onto the background if you prefer not to make stands.

fold

Whatcha need

- Large piece of unbleached muslin or a piece of white sheet
- Scissors
- Plastic drop cloth
- Tape
- Baby-food jars
- Food coloring
- Water
- Eye droppers
- Spray bottle for water
- Permanent markers

Altar Cloth

Whatcha do

1. Cut the cloth to fit your altar.
2. Place the cloth on top of the drop cloth.
3. Tape at various places around the edges.
4. Give each child a jar of food coloring mixed with water.
5. Use the eye droppers to drop spots of colored water on the cloth.
6. You may experiment with spraying the water on an area before and after dropping the colored water onto the cloth.
7. Allow the cloth to dry.
8. Use permanent markers to write a message on the cloth, such as "Jesus loves us," "He is risen!" or "Celebrate!"

Make a Mural

Butcher paper works

Well for the mural.

Whatcha need

Plain paper (three times the size of the Bible story picture), one piece per child

Bible story pictures (from Sunday school or vacation Bible school lesson leaflets)

Scissors

Glue or tape

Crayons or markers

Whatcha do

1. Cut the Bible story picture into four or five vertical sections (one section for each child in your class).
2. Cut the plain paper into the same number of strips.
3. Give each child one section of the Bible story picture and one strip of white paper.
4. Each student will use crayons or markers to reproduce their section of the Bible story picture onto the strip of white paper.
5. When all students have completed their pictures, glue or tape their sections together to form the mural. (You might want to tape the original Bible story picture together and hang it beside their mural to see the comparison and contrast.)

FOOD ACTIVITIES
AND RECIPES

Celebration Cake

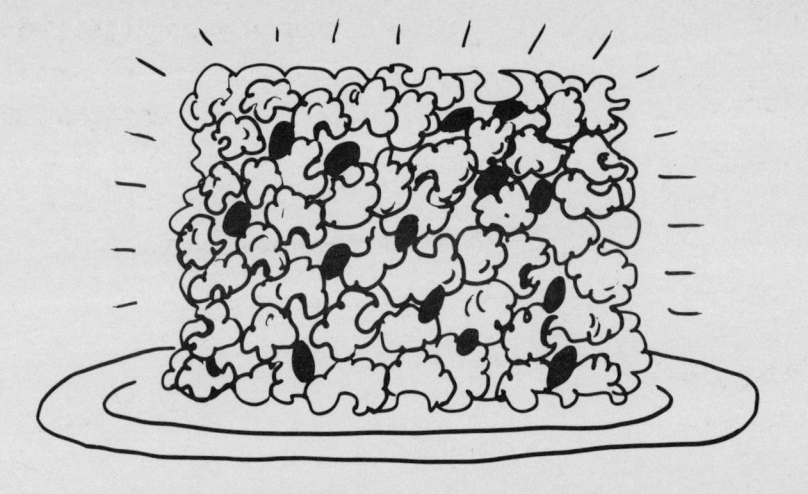

Whatcha need

- 6 quarts popcorn
- Cooking oil
- Popcorn popper
- 1 stick butter
- 1 large bag miniature marshmallows
- Gum drops or jelly beans, approximately 2 cups
- Angel food cake pan
- Nonstick cooking spray

Whatcha do

1. Pop the popcorn.
2. Separate the popped corn from the unpopped kernels. *Make sure there are no unpopped kernels left in the popcorn.*
3. Melt butter and marshmallows.
4. Add popcorn and jelly beans or gum drops. Mix well.
5. Spray the angel food cake pan with nonstick cooking spray.
6. Pat the popcorn and candy mixture firmly into the cake pan. Let cool.
7. Enjoy the celebration cake at a special resurrection or Baptism celebration.

Hint: Butter your hands lightly or use waxed paper to pat the popcorn and candy mixture into the cake pan so it won't stick to your hands.

Variation: Butter the children's hands. Each can make an individual popcorn ball to eat at their Easter celebration.

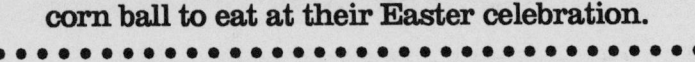

Caterpillar Cake

Whatcha need
- Cookie sheet
- Twinkies
- Cake doughnut
- Cool Whip (or other whipped topping)
- Green food coloring
- Plastic knives
- Jelly beans
- Licorice bites

Licorice bites

Twinkies

Jelly beans

Cool Whip

Whatcha do

1. Arrange the Twinkies on a cookie sheet according to the diagram to form a caterpillar. Place the cake doughnut for its head.
2. Color the Cool Whip with a few drops of green food coloring.
3. Ice the caterpillar with the green Cool Whip.
4. Arrange the jelly beans at the ends of each Twinkie to make feet; place licorice bites along the top of each Twinkie section.
5. Use candy pieces to make a face on the donut.

Note: Enjoy eating the caterpillar cake as you talk about God's creations, including all His critters, big and small.

Butterfly Cake

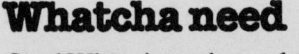

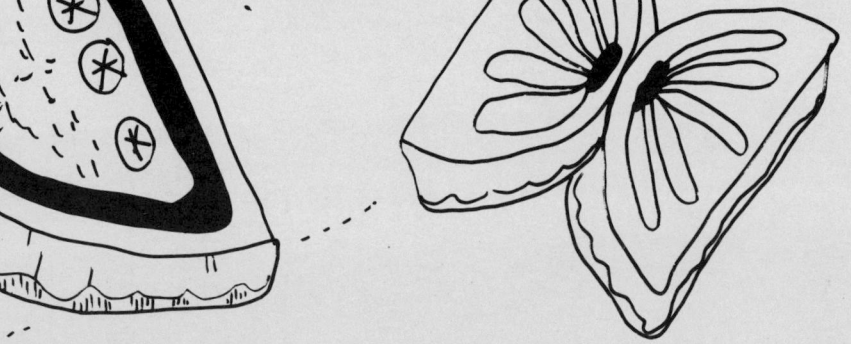

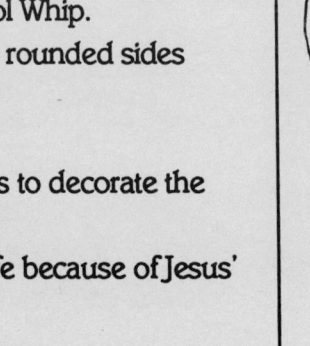

Whatcha need

Cool Whip (or other whipped topping)

Food coloring

Bowl

Round cake (1 layer)

Plastic knives

Licorice strings

Sprinkles

Candies

Whatcha do

1. Mix a few drops of food coloring into the Cool Whip.
2. Cut the cake in half. Place on a plate with the rounded sides together. See the diagram.
3. Frost the cake with the Cool Whip.
4. Use the licorice strings, sprinkles, and candies to decorate the butterfly.

Note: Use the butterfly cake to celebrate new life because of Jesus' resurrection.

Ice Cream, You Scream

Whatcha need

½ cup sugar

¼ teaspoon salt

1 cup milk

3 egg yolks, beaten

1 tablespoon vanilla

1 cup whipping cream

A 1-pound coffee can, with lid

Duct tape

A 3-pound coffee can, with lid

Crushed ice

Rock salt

Bowls

Spoons

Whatcha do

1. Blend sugar, salt, milk, and egg yolks. Cook at medium heat, stirring constantly.
2. Cook mixture until it comes to a boil. Remove from heat and cool.
3. Add vanilla and whipped cream.
4. Pour the mixture into a 1-pound coffee can. Tape the lid on tightly.
5. Put ½" of crushed ice into the bottom of the 3-pound coffee can.
6. Set the 1-pound can inside the 3-pound can; layer rock salt and crushed ice around the 1-pound can.
7. Tape the lid on the 3-pound can tightly.
8. In groups of four, roll the can back and forth for 15 minutes.
9. Open both cans. Gently stir the mixture. Tape the ice cream container shut again.
10. If needed, layer more ice and rock salt, tape the 3-pound can shut, and roll back and forth another 5–10 minutes.
11. Remove the lids. Enjoy the simple pleasures God gives us.

Note: You may want to sing favorite songs or work on Scripture memory while rolling the cans back and forth.

79

Blessing Cookies

Blessings

Jesus ♥ you.

You are special.

Hold the cookies to set the shape.

Whatcha need

- Typing paper (¹/₂" x 3" strips)
- Pencil
- Bible
- Electric skillet
- Vegetable oil spray
- Cookie batter
- Spatula

Cookie recipe: Mix 1 egg, ¹/₄ cup melted margarine, ²/₃ cup flour, ¹/₃ cup milk, ¹/₂ cup sugar, 1 teaspoon almond or orange flavoring, and ¹/₈ teaspoon salt. Batter will be thin. Preheat an electric skillet to 350 degrees. Keep children at a distance from the hot skillet.

Let your light shine.

...my peace I give you.

Whatcha do

1. Write blessings from God, God's promises, or Bible verses on the strips of paper.
2. Spray the skillet with vegetable oil.
3. Spoon batter into the skillet, making 1¹/₂"–2" circles. Cook three to four minutes. Watch carefully, and do not brown.
4. Remove the cookie from the skillet with the spatula. Add the strip of paper to the center and roll the cookie. Have someone hold the cookie while the next one is cooking in the skillet. This will give the cookie time to "set" the shape.
5. Share the blessing cookies with friends.

Edible Creations

Whatcha need

¹/₂ stick margarine (¹/₄ cup)

One 12-ounce bag miniature marshmallows

Favorite unsweetened cereal (8 cups)

Small candies and sprinkles

Waxed paper

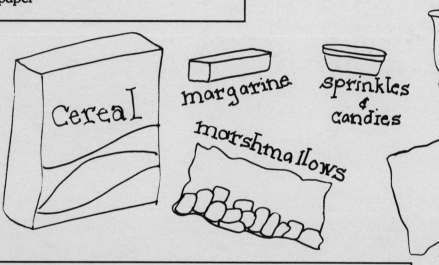

Cereal

margarine

sprinkles & candies

marshmallows

waxed paper

Whatcha do

1. Melt the margarine and marshmallows.
2. Mix the cereal and the marshmallows.
3. Sprinkle candies into the mixture.
4. While the mixture is warm, shape a creation on a piece of waxed paper.
5. Eat and enjoy as you talk about all the wonderful things God has made!

Options: Make a bird's nest and fill it with jelly beans; or make a basket, fish, heart, or butterfly.

Use a bowl to help form the basket.

Butter the children's hands before they work with the cereal.

Edible Play Dough and Pretzels

 Peanut butter

 Milk

 Pretzel Sticks

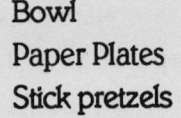

Cover the eating area with waxed paper or use paper plates.

Whatcha do

1. Wash hands before beginning.
2. Mix equal parts of dry milk and peanut butter.
3. Knead the dough until the mixture is a good consistency with which to work.
4. Shape dough into creatures and designs. Create interesting structures by adding stick pretzels. Enjoy!

Jesus Feeds 5,000

bread dough   margarine

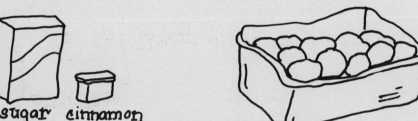

sugar   cinnamon

Whatcha need

One loaf of bread dough (you might want to use the
frozen bread dough from the grocer's freezer
section, but thaw it first)

Scissors (washed in hot water with soap)

One stick of margarine, melted (1/2 cup)

Cinnamon and sugar mixture

Bread loaf pan, oiled

Damp towel

butter, then cinnamon & sugar. Drop into the bread pan.

Dip the dough into the

Whatcha do

1. Cut the bread dough with scissors into very small pieces, approximately 1"- diameter sections.
2. Dip the bread dough pieces into the butter, then into a mixture of cinnamon and sugar.
3. Drop each piece into the pre-oiled bread pan.
4. Cover with a damp towel; let rise about 1 1/2 hours in a warm place.
5. Bake at 350 degrees for 1/2 hour, or until bread is browned. Check often.
6. Turn the pan of bread upside down on a plate.
7. Everyone can pull off a "bubble" of sweet bread to eat.

Note: Discuss how the yeast in the bread helped the dough to rise and bake into a big pan of bread. Talk about how Jesus miraculously made the bread multiply for the many hungry people that day on the hillside.

butter

cinnamon
& sugar

Try a Bundt pan.

83

LEARNING SCRIPTURE

Invisible Memory Review

Whatcha need
White paper
Waxed paper
Pencils
Bible

Whatcha do
1. Place a piece of waxed paper over a piece of white paper.
2. Write a favorite Bible verse or memory verse on the waxed paper. Press hard. Throw away the waxed paper.
3. Exchange white pieces of paper with another person.
4. Hold your pencil almost parallel to the paper. Rub your pencil over the sheet of paper.
5. Take turns reading each other's Bible verses.

Whatcha need
Chalkboard and chalk

Aa Bb Cc

For God   For God

Encourage the children to work as a group so all will feel success.

Whatcha do

Divide the class into two groups. They line up, facing the chalkboard. The first person on each team goes to the board to write the first word of the memory verse. The second person writes the second word. Continue this until the whole verse is written by a team.

Mix the children into different groups and repeat the activity.

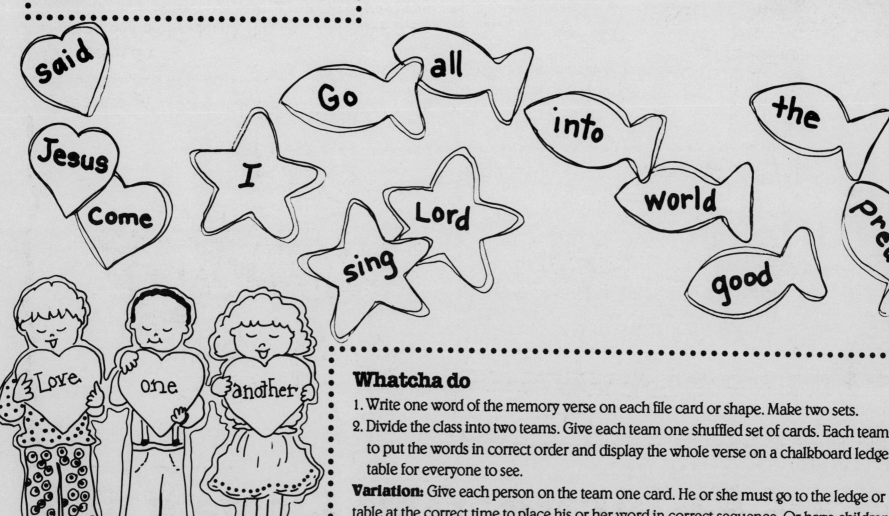

(hearts) Said, Jesus, Come

(hearts held by children) Love, one, another

(stars) I, sing, Lord

(fish) Go, all, into, world, the, good, preach

Whatcha do

1. Write one word of the memory verse on each file card or shape. Make two sets.
2. Divide the class into two teams. Give each team one shuffled set of cards. Each team is to put the words in correct order and display the whole verse on a chalkboard ledge or table for everyone to see.

Variation: Give each person on the team one card. He or she must go to the ledge or table at the correct time to place his or her word in correct sequence. Or have children stand and hold their words in the correct order.

Fun Memory Review

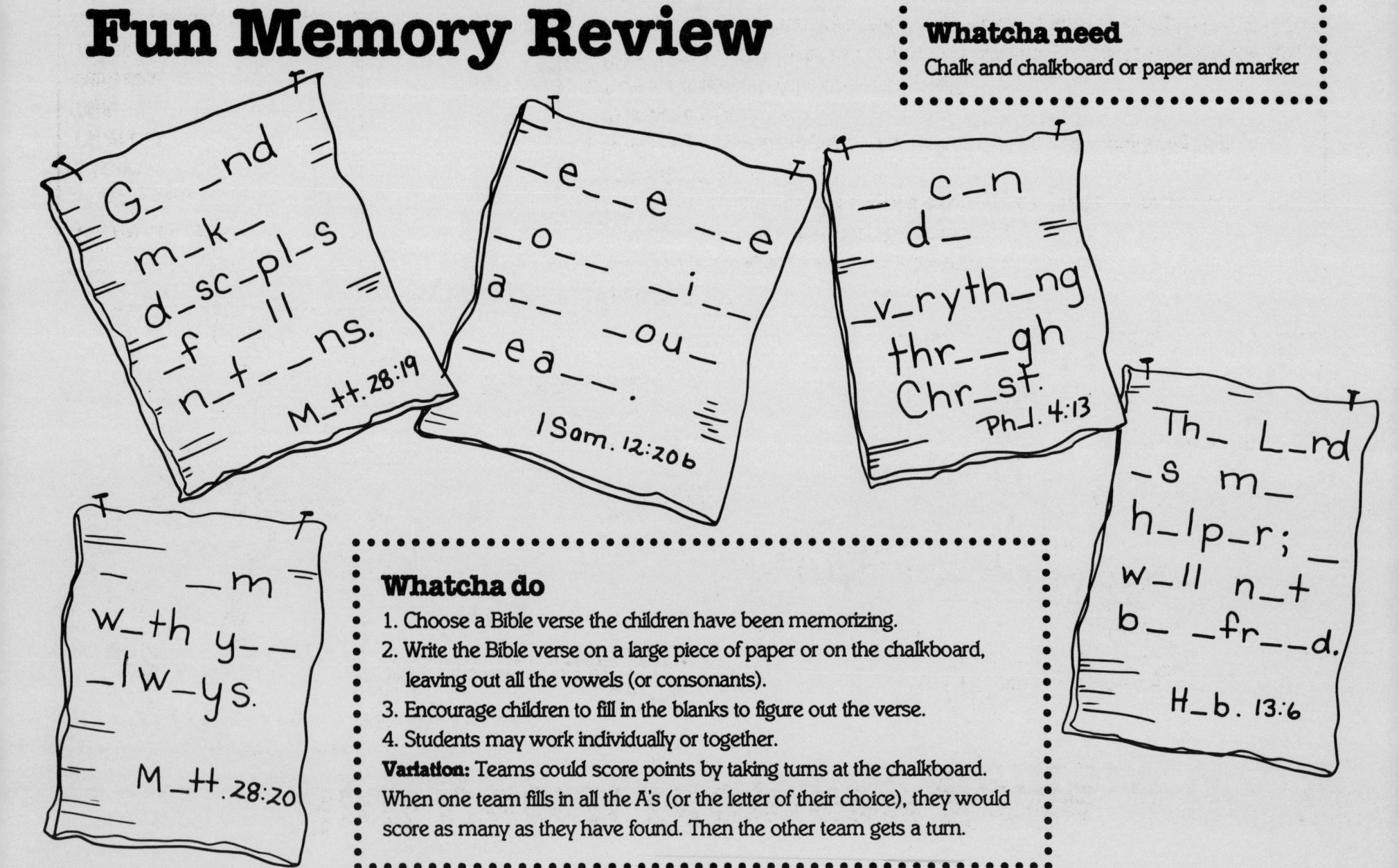

G_ _nd
m_k_
d_sc_pl_s
_f _ll
n_t_ _ns.

M_tt. 28:19

_e_ _e _ _e
_o_ _ _i_ _
a_ _ _ou_
_ea_ _.

1 Sam. 12:20b

_ _c_n
d_
_v_ryth_ng
thr_ _gh
Chr_st.

Ph_l. 4:13

Th_ L_rd
_s m_
h_lp_r; _
w_ll n_t
b_ _fr_ _d.

H_b. 13:6

_ _ _m
w_th y_ _
_lw_ys.

M_tt. 28:20

Whatcha do

1. Choose a Bible verse the children have been memorizing.
2. Write the Bible verse on a large piece of paper or on the chalkboard, leaving out all the vowels (or consonants).
3. Encourage children to fill in the blanks to figure out the verse.
4. Students may work individually or together.

Variation: Teams could score points by taking turns at the chalkboard. When one team fills in all the A's (or the letter of their choice), they would score as many as they have found. Then the other team gets a turn.

Ball Catch Memory Race

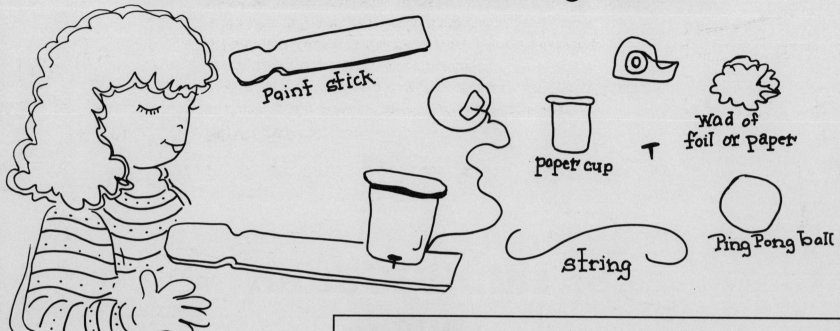

Paint stick

paper cup

Wad of foil or paper

string

Ping Pong ball

Whatcha need

String or yarn
Scissors
Paper cup
Tape
Paint stick
Thumbtack
Scrap paper, aluminum foil,
   or Ping-Pong ball

Whatcha do

1. Measure the string at about the length of your arm, and cut it.
2. Tape one end of the string to the base of the paper cup.
3. Tack the paper cup onto the end of the paint stick so that it sits on the end of the stick.
4. Wad up a piece of scrap paper or aluminum foil (or use a Ping-Pong ball) to fit into the cup.
5. Tape the other end of the string to the ball.
6. Now practice catching the ball in the cup. Each time you catch the ball in the cup, say a word of your memory verse. See how quickly you can complete the whole verse.

PATTERNS
and
REPRODUCIBLES

Words of Promise

Look up the Bible verses to find God's words of promise.

James 5:15

Genesis 9:13

Psalm 135:4

John 1:41

Colossians 3:24

Luke 2:11

1 John 5:13

P R A Y E R

P
R
O
M
I
S
E

91

Promise Word Search

In this word search you will find 28 words and names
relating to promises God tells us in the Bible.
The words you are to find are listed in the box.
Circle each word in the word search puzzle.

PROMISE	HEAVEN
DREAM	SALVATION
RESURRECTION	BAPTISM
BREAD	FORGIVENESS
ABRAHAM	MARY
NOAH	LIFE
RAINBOW	PEACE
JESUS	JOY
HEZEKIAH	MARTHA
LOVE	JACOB
BELIEVE	STORM
PRAYER	JAIL
HEALING	PAUL
SHEPHERD	SILAS

```
P R A Y E R B B S D V S A
R A F R S A S R H F Y E B
O L O A M J A I L I B P R
M A R T H A H A E L E E A
I C G C T C R L L N O A H
S Z I D S O L Y U R H C A
E Y V H M B R E A D J E M
L B E L I E V E P R M L U
S E N I S M M T J E S U S
H H E A L I N G O A I B E
E I S S O N L Z Y M C R T
P J S H V S E A B H N O C
H E A V E N S S S A X J B
E M E L L Z H H L T G C G
R E S U R R E C T I O N W
D R L M R G T K O K F R F
C S K G B A P T I S M E M
B R A I N B O W K A S B H
S A L V A T I O N C H Q A
```

Words of RPSIAE

Unscramble the words of praise:

thank you	Father	please
praise	pray	worship
kneel	hands	guidance
Jesus	ask	love
blessed	forever	exalt

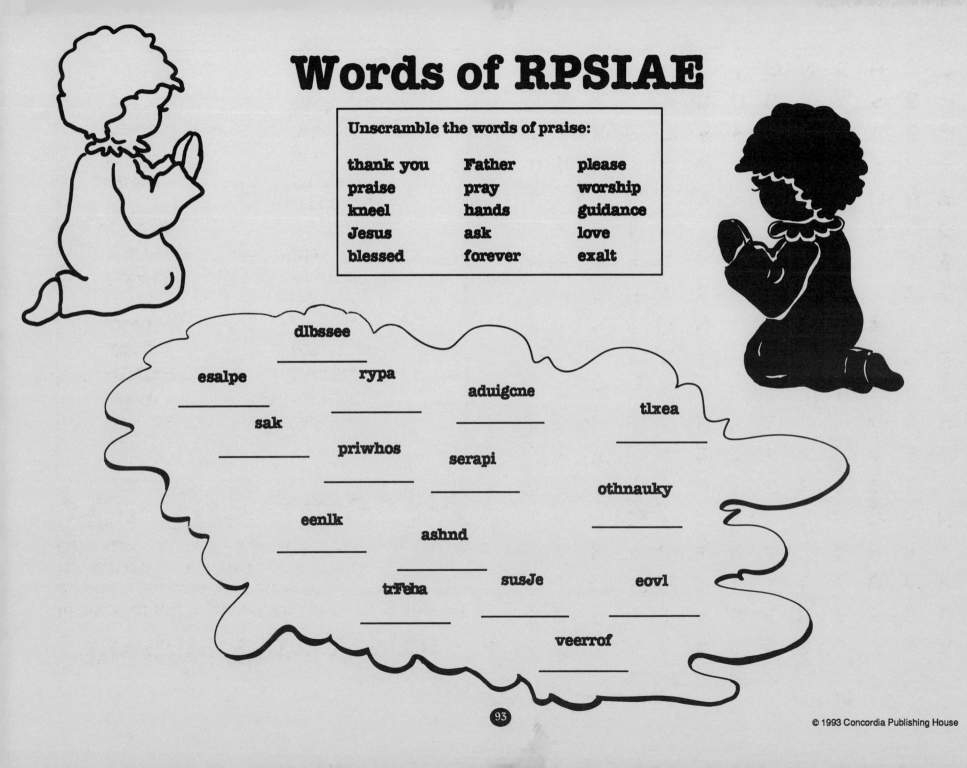

dlbssee

_____

esalpe   rypa

_____   aduigcne

sak   tlxea

priwhos   serapi   _____

_____   othnauky

eenlk   ashnd   _____

_____

trFeha   susJe   eovl

_____   _____

veerrof

_____

Computer Message 1

Follow the arrows from letter to letter to read the message
found in **Hebrews 10:23.**
Print each letter of the message in order on the lines below.

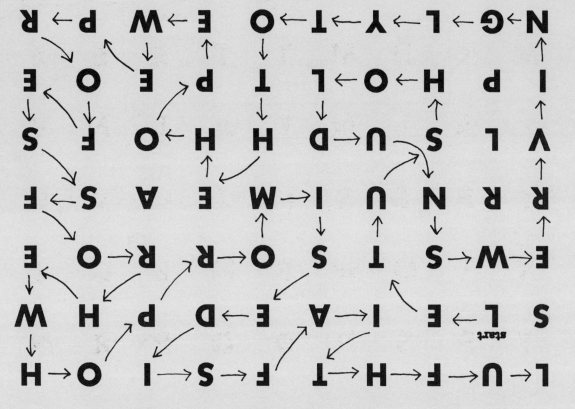

start

LET __ __ ___ ___ __ ___ ___ ___ ___ ___

___ ___ __ ___ ___ , ___ ___ __ ___ ___ ___

___ ___ ___ ___ ___ __ ___ ___ __ ___ .

Computer Message 2

Draw arrows from one letter to another to complete the computer message found in **1 John 2:25**.

Start

A F P M L P M Y T E E E A Y P

N E I L A A N E A L N V S U D

D T H I S T R H T H V B R E Q

O R L K I O W B N E O I S B P

L G K T P S P D O P R M Q N T

___ ____ ___ __ ____

__ _____ ___ _

____ _____ ____.   **1 John 2:25**

Prayer Acrostic

1. Cross out all the names used in the Bible for *God*.
2. Cross out words of things for which we *pray*.
3. Cross out words that have *double consonants*.
4. Cross out names of *Biblical women*.
5. Cross out names of the *colors of the rainbow*.

Jahweh	Ruth	healing	Bathsheba	thankful
balloon	being	Savior	class	green
food	guidance	yellow	devote	clothing
Esther	red	Jehovah	Mary	Rebekah
to	and	pattern	peace	blue
orange	indigo	violet	watchful	Messiah
Emmanuel	Sarah	prayer	Christ	yourselves

The words remaining come from **Colossians 4:2**.

See if you can put the remaining words in correct order
before checking your answer in the book of Colossians.

_____

_____

Which Picture? Which Bible Story? 1

Draw a line from the name of the Bible story to the matching picture.

1. Jesus Feeds 5,000

2. Jesus' Crucifixion and Resurrection

3. The Jailer at Philippi

4. Paul Shipwrecked on Malta

5. Jacob's Wonderful Dream

Which Picture? Which Bible Story? 2

Match the picture with the Bible story. Draw a line to connect the matches.

1. The Baptism of Jesus

2. The Forgiving Father

3. Jesus Heals a Paralyzed Man

4. Mary and Martha

5. King Hezekiah Prays

Bible Mates—Who Am I?

In each blank space, print the name of the husband or wife.

Husbands

Adam	Zechariah
Jacob	David
Joseph	Samson
Boaz	Abraham
Isaac	

Wives

Ruth	Delilah
Rebekah	Elizabeth
Rachel	Sarah
Mary	Bathsheba
Eve	

_____ 1. I had to work hard to come up with names for all those animals.

_____ 2. God gave me a test for which I could not study.

_____ 3. I thought boys might be cheaper by the dozen.

_____ 4. My son had two fathers.

_____ 5. I am known as a "good" king.

_____ 6. My hair brought me down.

_____ 7. My twin sons fought about their birthright.

_____ 8. I left wheat in the fields for others to gather.

_____ 9. I became speechless until my son was born.

_____ 1. I'm known as the "first lady."

_____ 2. One of my husbands was killed in the front line of duty.

_____ 3. My laugh got me in trouble with the Lord.

_____ 4. I went to a well to get water, and came back with a husband.

_____ 5. It was important that my son be born before Jesus.

_____ 6. I was specially chosen by God.

_____ 7. I gathered the wheat grains from the fields.

_____ 8. My sister and I shared a husband.

_____ 9. You might say I was a poor hair stylist.

Match the couples by writing in the correct wife's name:

Adam and _____

Abraham and _____

Isaac and _____

Jacob and _____

Samson and _____

Boaz and _____

David and _____

Zechariah and _____

Joseph and _____

God Answers Prayer

Fill in the boxes with the following words of prayer.

Three examples have been done for you. You'll need to use those three words again.

God	answers	prayer	Savior
call	believe	exalt	comfort
deeds	praise	ever	
song	altar	adore	

G O D

A N S W E R S

P R A Y E R

Decode the Prayer Passage

In each space, print the letter of the alphabet that comes *after* the letter given.
To check your answer, read **Psalm 6:9**.

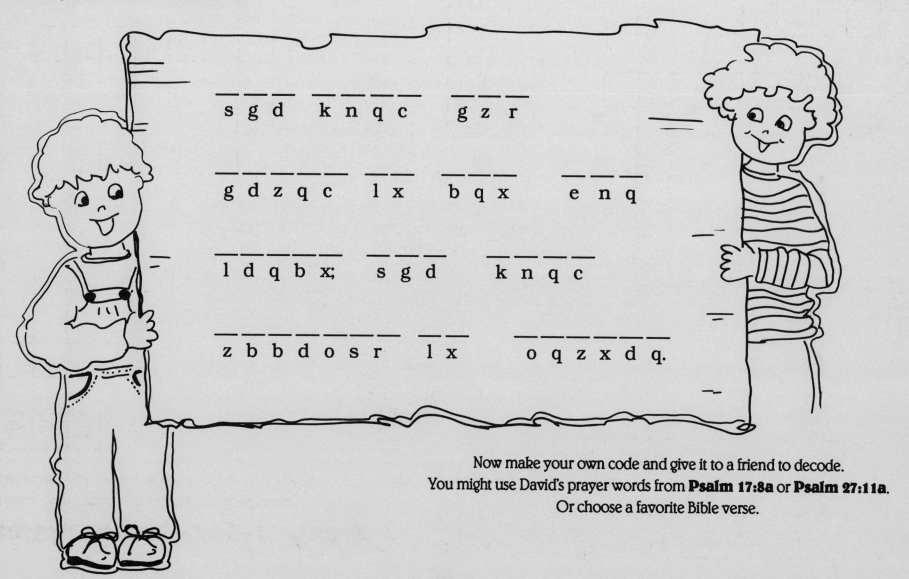

___ ___ ___   ___ ___ ___ ___   ___ ___ ___
 s   g   d   k   n   q   c   g   z   r

___ ___ ___ ___ ___   ___ ___   ___ ___ ___   ___ ___ ___
 g   d   z   q   c   l   x   b   q   x   e   n   q

___ ___ ___ ___ ___;   ___ ___ ___   ___ ___ ___ ___
 l   d   q   b   x;   s   g   d   k   n   q   c

___ ___ ___ ___ ___ ___ ___   ___ ___   ___ ___ ___ ___ ___ ___ ___.
 z   b   b   d   o   s   r   l   x   o   q   z   x   d   q.

Now make your own code and give it to a friend to decode.
You might use David's prayer words from **Psalm 17:8a** or **Psalm 27:11a**.
Or choose a favorite Bible verse.

Is or Not

Decode the sentences to find the special message.

My first letter is in **good** but not in **food**. ____

My second letter is in **open** but not in **pencil**. ____

My third letter is in **day** but not in **play**. ____

My first letter is in **ask** but not in **sky**. ____

My second letter is in **chain** but not in **chair**. ____

My third letter is in **animals** but not in **animal**. ____

My fourth letter is in **whole** but not in **hole**. ____

My fifth letter is in **plane** but not in **plan**. ____

My sixth letter is in **start** but not in **state**. ____

My seventh letter is in **save** but not in **cave**. ____

My first letter is in **page** but not in **cage**. ____

My second letter is in **pray** but not in **pay**. ____

My third letter is in **apple** but not in **people**. ____

My fourth letter is in **carry** but not in **cart**. ____

My fifth letter is in **aster** but not in **star**. ____

My sixth letter is in **pretty** but not in **type**. ____

_ _ _   _ _ _ _ _ _   _ _ _ _ _ _ .

God's Messages to Us

God has given an important message to us in each of the following Bible stories.
Match the story with God's message.

Jesus Feeds 5,000

Believe and be saved.

Jesus' Crucifixion and Resurrection

Even when we disobey God, He will protect us.

The Jailer at Philippi

I will take care of you and give you your daily needs.

Paul Shipwrecked on Malta

God will make us strong even when Satan tempts us and sends us trouble.

Jacob's Wonderful Dream

Because of what Jesus has done, we can be God's children.

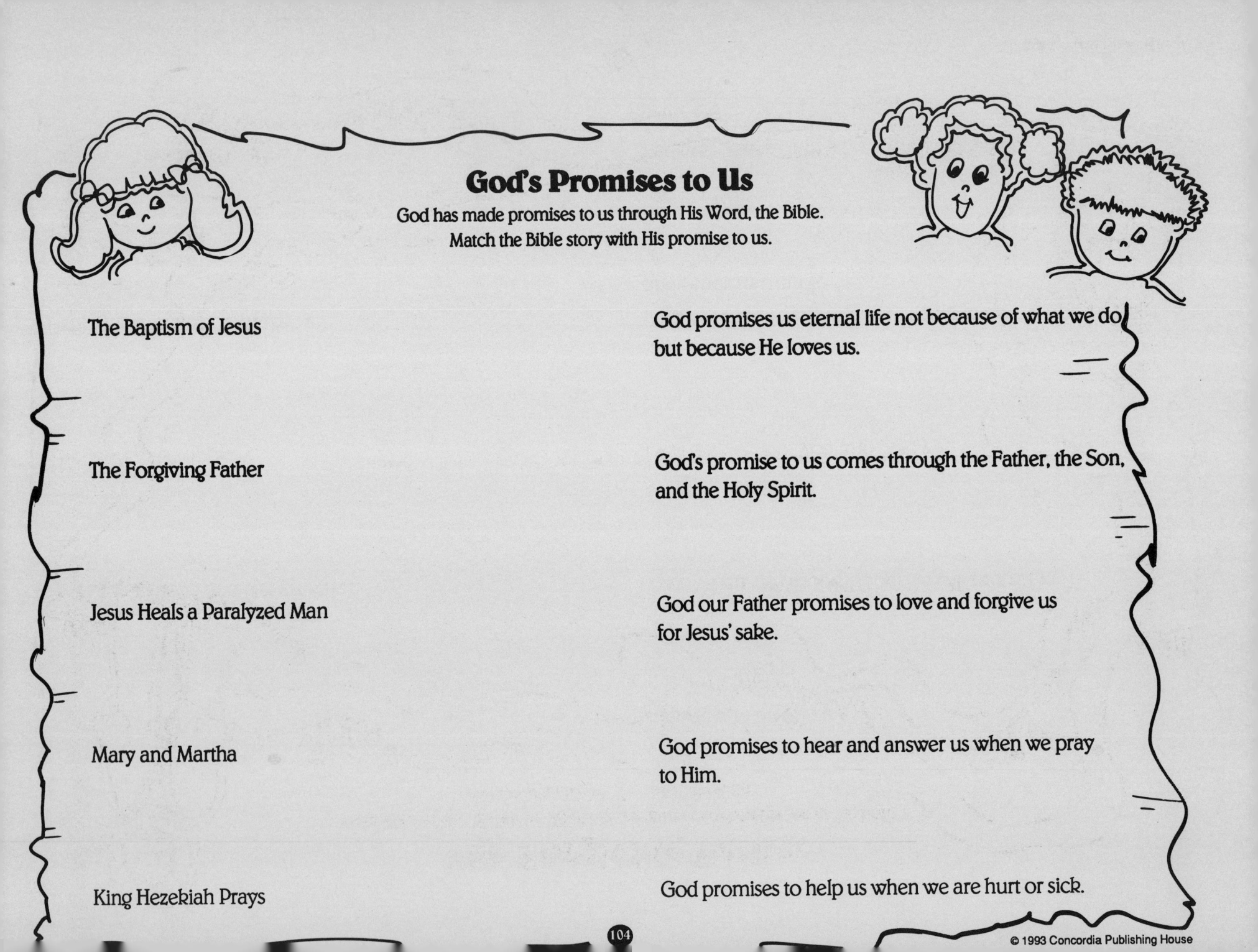

God's Promises to Us

God has made promises to us through His Word, the Bible.
Match the Bible story with His promise to us.

The Baptism of Jesus

God promises us eternal life not because of what we do but because He loves us.

The Forgiving Father

God's promise to us comes through the Father, the Son, and the Holy Spirit.

Jesus Heals a Paralyzed Man

God our Father promises to love and forgive us for Jesus' sake.

Mary and Martha

God promises to hear and answer us when we pray to Him.

King Hezekiah Prays

God promises to help us when we are hurt or sick.

The Forgiving Father

Help the son find his father. What did the father do when his son came home?
Draw a picture of their celebration.

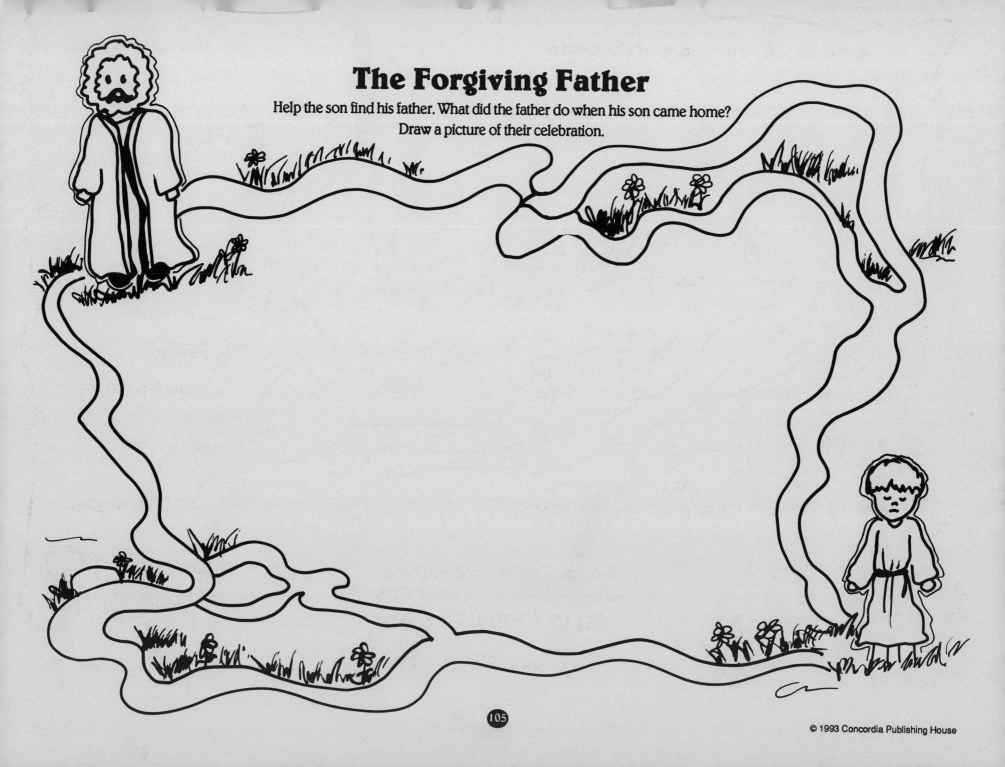

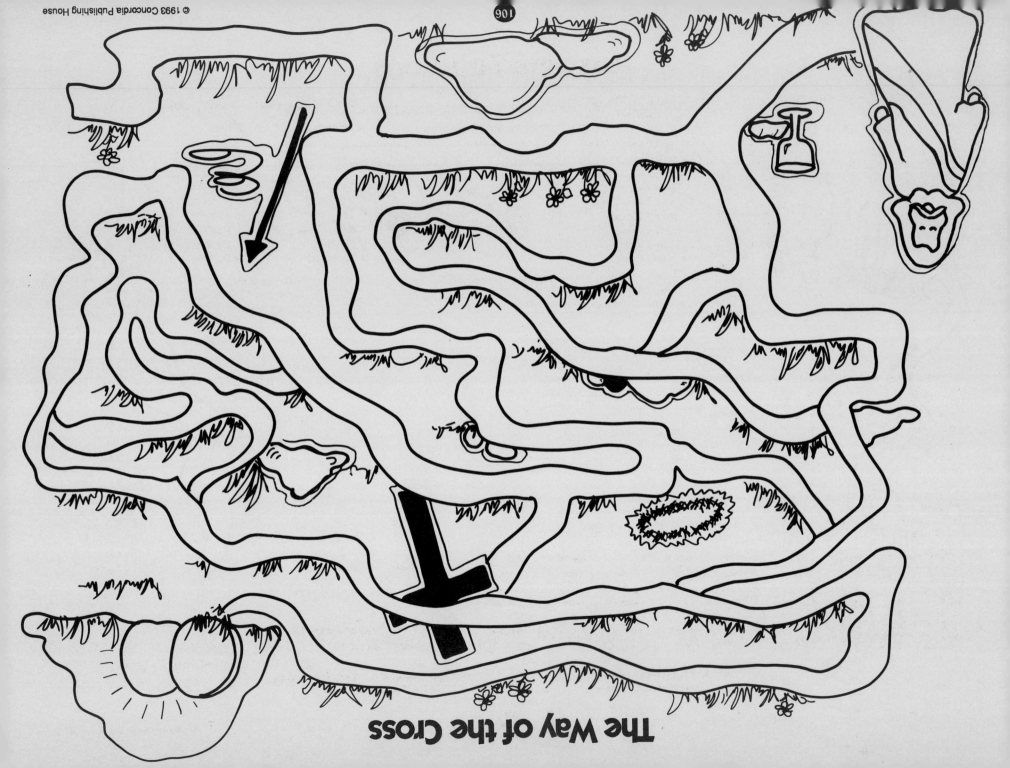

The Way of the Cross

Answers/Solutions

Words of Promise (p. 91)

P	R	O	M	I	S	E
Prayer	Rainbow	Own	Messiah	Inheritance	Savior	Eternal life

Words of RPSIAE (p. 93)

rypa = pray
sak = ask
aduigcne = guidance
serapi = praise
othnauky = thank-you
eenlk = kneel
priwhos = worship
ashnd = hands
trFeha = Father
esalpe = please
susJe = Jesus
dlbssee = blessed
eovl = love
veerrof = forever
tlxea = exalt

Computer Message 1 (p. 94)

Let us hold unswervingly to the hope we profess, for He who promised is faithful.

Computer Message 2 (p. 95)

And this is what He promised us—even eternal life.

Promise Word Search (p. 92)

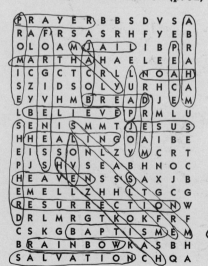

Prayer Acrostic (p. 96)

Jahweh — balloon — food — Esther — to — orange — Emmanuel
Ruth — being — guidance — red — and — indigo — Sarah
healing — Savior — yellow — Jehovah — pattern — violet — prayer
Bathsheba — class — devote — clothing — Rebekah — blue — Messiah — Christ
thankful — green — clothing — Rebekah — blue — Messiah — yourselves

Devote yourselves to prayer, being watchful and thankful.

Bible Mates—Who Am I? (p. 99)

Husbands	Wives
1. Adam	1. Eve
2. Abraham	2. Bathsheba
3. Jacob	3. Sarah
4. Joseph	4. Rebekah
5. David	5. Elizabeth
6. Samson	6. Mary
7. Isaac	7. Ruth
8. Boaz	8. Rachel
9. Zechariah	9. Delilah

Adam and Eve
Abraham and Sarah
Isaac and Rebekah
Jacob and Rachel
Samson and Delilah
Boaz and Ruth
David and Bathsheba
Zechariah and Elizabeth
Joseph and Mary

God Answers Prayer (p. 100)

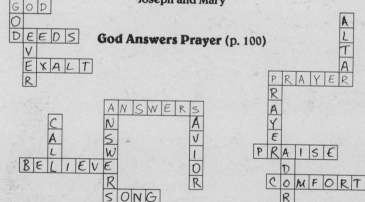

Decode the Prayer Passage, Psalm 6:9 (p. 101)

The Lord has heard my cry for mercy; the Lord accepts my prayer.

Is or Not (p. 102)

God Answers Prayer

God's Messages to Us (p. 103)

Jesus Feeds 5,000	Believe and be saved.
Jesus' Crucifixion and Resurrection	Even when we disobey God, He will protect us.
The Jailer at Philippi	I will take care of you and give you your daily needs.
Paul Shipwrecked on Malta	God will make us strong even when Satan tempts us and sends us trouble.
Jacob Wonderful Dream	Because of what Jesus has done, we can be God's children.

God's Promises to Us (p. 104)

The Baptism of Jesus	God promises us eternal life not because of what we do but because He loves us.
The Forgiving Father	God's promise to us comes through the Father, the Son, and the Holy Spirit.
Jesus Heals a Paralyzed Man	God our Father promises to love and forgive us for Jesus' sake.
Mary and Martha	God promises to hear and answer us when we pray to Him.
King Hezekiah Prays	God promises to help us when we are hurt or sick.

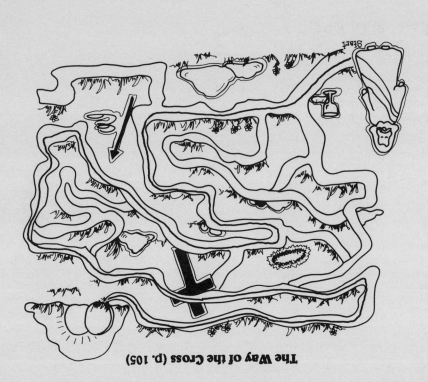

The Way of the Cross (p. 105)

PATTERN SHEETS

The butterfly represents New Life and reminds us of Christ's resurrection.

and creativity

The fish is a secret symbol used by early Christians to tell others they believed in Christ.

The Holy Spirit

---encourage individuality

the star led the wisemen to the Christ child.

a shepherd's staff

Encourage children to make their own patterns or if they use these patterns---

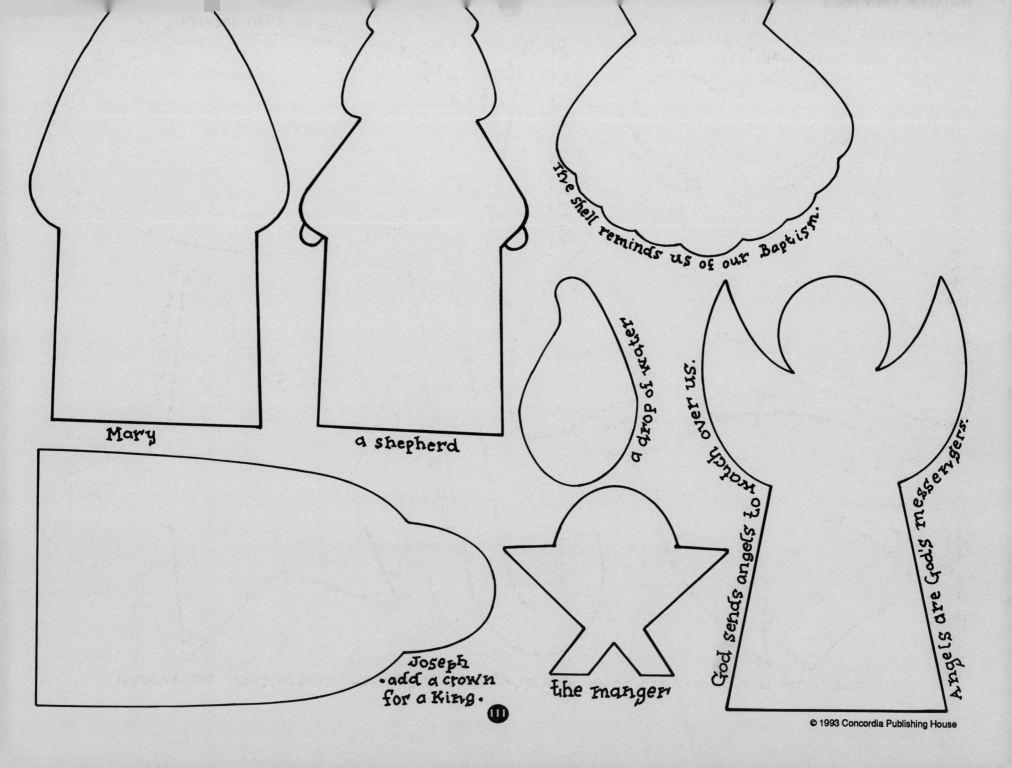

Mary

a shepherd

The shell reminds us of our Baptism.

a drop of water

Joseph
•add a crown
for a King.

the manger

God sends angels to watch over us.

Angels are God's messengers.

111

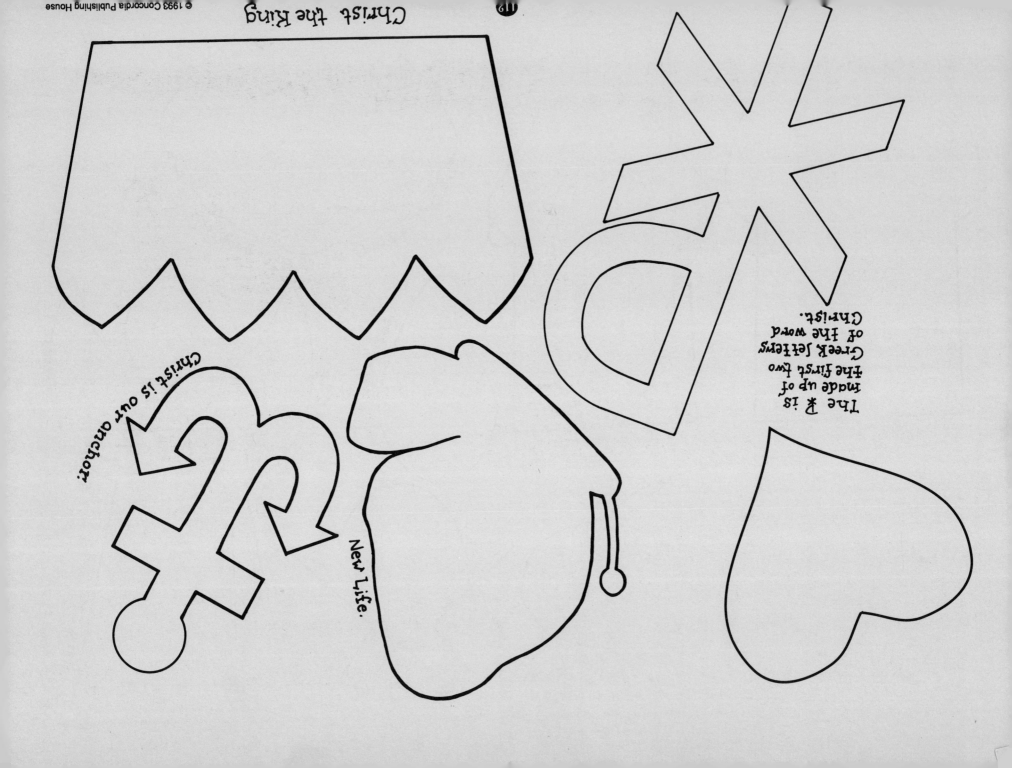

112

The ☧ is made up of the first two Greek letters of the word Christ.

Christ is our anchor.

New Life.